MENTAL ILLNESS AND PSYCHOLOGY

MENTAL ILLNESS

and

PSYCHOLOGY

Michel Foucault

Translated by Alan Sheridan
Foreword by Hubert Dreyfus

University of California Press
Berkeley   Los Angeles   London

University of California Press
Berkeley and Los Angeles

University of California Press, Ltd.
London, England

This work was first published in French under the title *Maladie Mentale et Personalité*. © 1954 by Presses Universitaires de France.

Revised and republished as *Maladie Mentale et Psychologie*.
© 1962 by Presses Universitaires de France.

English translation of *Maladie Mentale et Psychologie* copyright © 1976
by Harper & Row, Publishers, Inc.

First University of California Press paperback edition published 1987.
Published by arrangement with Harper & Row, Publishers, Inc. All rights reserved.

Library of Congress Cataloging-in-Publication Data

Foucault, Michel.
    Mental illness and psychology.

    Translation of Maladie mentale et psychologie.
    1. Mental illness. I. Title.
RC454.F6513   1987   616.89   86-30900
ISBN 0-520-05919-0 (alk. paper)

Printed in the United States of America

1   2   3   4   5   6   7   8   9

Contents

Foreword to the California Edition

In the original version of the introduction to *The Use of Pleasure,* Michel Foucault offers a lucid retrospective account of the project and the problems of his first book, *Mental Illness and Psychology.*

To study forms of experience... —in their history—is an idea that originated with an earlier project, in which I made use of the methods of existential analysis in the field of psychiatry and in the domain of "mental illness". For two reasons, not unrelated to each other, this project left me unsatisfied: its theoretical weakness in elaborating the notion of experience, and its ambiguous link with a psychiatric practice which it simultaneously ignored and took for granted. One could deal with the first problem by referring to a general theory of the human being, and treat the second altogether differently by turning, as is so often done, to the "economic and social context"; one could choose, by doing so, to accept the resulting dilemma of a philosophical anthropology and a social history. But I wondered whether, rather than playing on this alternative, it would not be possible to consider the very historicity of forms of experience. This entailed two negative tasks:

first, a "nominalist" reduction of philosophical anthropology and
the notions which it serves to promote, and second, a shift of domain to the concepts and methods of the history of societies.[1]

In this passage Foucault refers to *Mental Illness and
Psychology* obliquely, not by its title, and this whole paragraph is
deleted in the final version of the introduction. Clearly, Foucault
did not like the book. He left a note categorically refusing all
reprint rights to the first version,[2] published in 1954, just two
years after he received his Diplôme de Psycho-Pathologie from
the University of Paris, and he tried unsuccessfully to prevent the
translation of the radically revised 1962 version, presented here.[3]
The cryptic account quoted above refers to both these versions:
the first, an unstable combination of Heideggerian existential anthropology and Marxist social history; the second, with the social
history replaced with a history of forms of experience. Foucault
had good reasons for distancing himself from both, yet both versions contain important preoccupations, as well as weapons and
targets that were to remain with Foucault all his life.

In this brief introduction to *Mental Illness and Psychology*
Foucault raises two questions: "Under what conditions can one
speak of illness in the psychological domain?" and "What relations can one define between the facts of mental pathology and
those of organic pathology?" (p. 1).[4] In the first version, each
part of the two-part book was meant to answer one of these questions. In both versions Part I does answer question one, but in
1962 the original Part II, "The Actual Conditions of Illness,"
which offered a Marxist account of mental illness and a Pavlovian account of its organic basis, was replaced by a new Part II,
"Madness and Culture," which is a summary of Foucault's
Madness and Civilization, published in 1961. It addresses not the
social and organic basis of mental pathology but rather examines
the cultural basis of the very idea of mental pathology. Foucault
thus switches from an account of the *social* conditions that *cause*
mental illness to the *cultural* conditions that lead us to *treat*

madness as mental illness. He modifies his introduction accord-
ingly. Rather than offering "a reflection on man himself," he
proposes "to show that the root of mental pathology must be
sought not in some kind of 'metapathology,' but in a certain
relation, historically situated, of man to the madman and to the
true man" (p. 2).

What remains constant through both versions and throughout
Foucault's life, however, is his debt to recent postphilosophical
modes of thought typified by Martin Heidegger, especially
Heidegger's aversion to claims, exemplified by Sigmund Freud, to
provide a science of the human subject. In his last interview
Foucault said of Heidegger: "For me Heidegger has always been
the essential philosopher. . . . I set out to read Heidegger in 1951
or 1952. . . . My entire philosophical development was determined
by my reading of Heidegger."[5] So it is not surprising that Part I
of *Mental Illness and Psychology,* which remained relatively un-
changed in both versions, can be read as a critique of psychoanalysis using the ideas of Ludwig Binswanger,[6] who in turn based
his phenomenological therapy on the notion of being-in-the-
world worked out in Heidegger's *Being and Time;*[7] while the new
Part II combines early Heideggerian hermeneutics with a variation on Heidegger's later account of the stages by which the
Western understanding of being covered up the truth of being,
thereby situating psychoanalysis as the culmination of a systematic cover-up and exclusion of the true meaning of madness.

Mental Illness and Psychology is thus the opening salvo in
Foucault's lifelong use of the interpretation of practices against
the claims of the human sciences. The basic idea of Part I of both
the first and second versions is that whereas organic medicine is a
genuine science of the body, there cannot be a similar science of
human beings. "My aim," Foucault tells us, "is to show that
mental pathology requires methods of analysis different from
those of organic pathology and that it is only by an artifice of
language that the same meaning can be attributed to 'illnesses of
the body' and 'illnesses of the mind' "(p. 10).

According to Foucault, when organic pathology gave up treating specific diseases as natural kinds—each caused by a specific agent—and introduced a new notion of the body as an organic unity disrupted by disease, it became scientific. Anatomy and physiology provide "an analysis that authorizes valid abstractions against the background of organic totality. . . . The importance given in organic pathology to the notion of totality excludes neither the abstraction of isolated elements nor causal analysis; on the contrary, it makes possible a more valid abstraction and the determination of a more real causality" (p. 10).

But, Foucault argues, while a theoretical, causal account of the normal and abnormal functions of relatively isolable subsystems and organisms is being achieved in organic medicine, a parallel scientific approach has not succeeded in psychiatry. When psychologists such as Kurt Goldstein tried to extend the holistic approach that worked in organic medicine to an account of the personality as an aspect of the organism, they extended the idea beyond its proper domain. Foucault writes of the attempt to combine organic pathology and mental pathology: "The unity that such a metapathology provides between the various forms of illness is never more than factitious" (p. 13).[8]

Given Foucault's later concern with "truth-effects" rather than truth-claims, one might suppose that Foucault later abandoned his claim that organic medicine realized "the determination of . . . real causality" (p. 10). But Foucault would then no longer have been able to distinguish a psychiatry modeled on medicine—especially psychoanalytical theory, which he treats as a pseudoscience throughout his works—from valid theories in the natural and biological sciences, since in that case every science that made causal claims would be equally self-deluded. Therefore one should not be surprised to find that despite his interest in the historical background and social consequences of all truth-claims, Foucault remained throughout his life a scientific realist in the tradition of his teacher, Georges Canguilhem. In an appreciation of the work of Canguilhem, Foucault wrote in 1985:

"In the history of science one cannot take truth as given, but neither can one do without a relation to the truth and to the opposition of the true and the false. It is this reference to the order of the true and the false which gives to that history its specificity and its importance."[9] When, in *The Archaeology of Knowledge,* Foucault notes the thresholds of positivity, epistemologization, scientificity, and formalization through which discursive formations pass,[10] he is speaking of stages of the rationalization of the physical sciences as seen by a long tradition of French philosophers from Comte to Duhem to Bachelard to Althusser. According to this view, some sciences, such as physics, presumably because their techniques of investigation put them in touch with an independent causal reality, free themselves from the power practices in which they originate and gain autonomy and objectivity, while others, whose techniques are not appropriate to their objects, are stuck with methods dictated not by their subject matter but by the power practices under which they were developed. In *Discipline and Punish,* a relatively late work, Foucault still contrasts the natural and the human sciences in this way. After discussing the early dependence of natural science on the techniques of the inquisition and of psychology on the examination, Foucault notes that "although it is true that, in becoming a technique for the empirical sciences, the investigation has detached itself from the inquisitorial procedure, in which it was historically rooted, the [psychological] examination has remained extremely close to the disciplinary power that shaped it."[11]

Later Foucault is interested exclusively in the nonautonomous human sciences and the way they have remained involved with power. Therefore he says nothing more about the autonomous natural ones. It seems reasonable to suppose, however, that Foucault retained the view stated in this first book that the natural sciences have been able to arrive at relative autonomy because they have found a level of analysis that authorizes valid abstractions corresponding to the causal powers in the physical world.

Not only does Foucault, in *Mental Illness and Psychology,* claim that organic medicine achieved autonomy but, in the same passage, he implies that such autonomy is impossible for the sciences of man. According to Foucault, following Binswanger and the existential therapists, the personality cannot be grasped as an organic totality of isolable functional components. The unity is much tighter. Each aspect of behavior can only be understood as an expression of an individual's basic way of being-in-the-world, or what Sartre calls a "fundamental project."

> Now, psychology has never been able to offer psychiatry what physiology gave to medicine: a tool of analysis that, in delimiting the disorder, makes it possible to envisage the functional relationship of this damage to the personality as a whole. The coherence of a psychological life seems, in effect, to be assured in some way other than the cohesion of an organism; the integration of its segments tends toward a unity that makes each possible, but that is compressed and gathered together in each: this is what psychologists call, in the vocabulary that they have borrowed from phenomenology, the significant unity of behavior, which contains in each element—dream, crime, gratuitous gesture, free association—the general appearance, the style, the whole historical anteriority and possible implications, of an existence.   (pp. 10-11)

The moral of Chapter 1, then, is that the natural sciences can be right about the functional components of physical and organic nature but there is no human nature for the human sciences to be right about. There is no reason to think that Foucault ever abandoned this plausible position that parallels Heidegger's and Canguilhem's account of the relation of the natural and human sciences.[12]

Consequently, in Chapter 2 Foucault considers and rejects a recent theory of human nature, psychological evolutionism, with its account of neurosis as fixation at an early, primitive, infantile stage of the development of the libido. As Foucault puts it, for Freud "every libidinal stage is a potential pathological structure. Neurosis is a spontaneous archaeology of the libido" (p. 21).

Foucault sees this view as based on "the myth, to begin with, of a certain psychological substance (Freud's 'libido,' Janet's 'psychic force'), which is seen as the raw material of evolution and which, progressing in the course of individual and social development, is subject to relapses and can fall back, through illness, to an earlier state; the myth, too, of an identity between the mentally ill person, the primitive, and the child" (p. 24). He rejects this view in the name of the specificity of the sick person: "There can be no question . . . of archaic personalities; we must accept the specificity of the morbid personality; the pathological structure of the psyche is not a return to origins; it is strictly original" (pp. 25–26).

Foucault is saying, in effect, that where human beings are concerned, perspicuous description must replace (pseudo) scientific explanation: "Regression, therefore, must be taken as only one of the descriptive aspects of mental illness. . . . This would not involve explaining pathological structures, but simply placing them in a perspective that would make the facts of individual or social regression observed by Freud . . . coherent and comprehensible" (p. 26).

A descriptive, i.e., phenomenological, approach reveals that developmental accounts modeled on nature leave out the way the sick patient structures his world and gives meaning to his past. "Regression is not a natural falling back into the past; it is an intentional [i.e., meaningful but not necessarily consciously chosen] flight from the present" (p. 33). To understand pathology we must turn to the patient's personal history. "Freud's stroke of genius lay in being able . . . to go beyond the evolutionist horizon defined by the notion of libido and reach the historical dimension of the human psyche" (p. 31).

In Chapter 3 Foucault sketches this historical dimension. The conscientious recent Ph.D. bends over backward to do justice to Freud and in so doing, for the last time in his writings, appropriates Freudian terminology. He speaks with professional precision and implicit agreement of repression, reversal, castration fear, projection, and the Oedipal situation; he even seems to accept a sexual account of motivation and symbolic fulfillment. But he draws the line at "the biological reality of a paradoxical 'death instinct' " (p. 34). What he accepts from Freud is not his pseudobiological account of the production of symptoms. He focuses rather on how psychoanalytic concern shifted from an emphasis on a causal explanation of symptoms to a description of styles of defenses:

> This notion of psychological defense is of major importance. The whole of psychoanalysis has centered around it. An investigation of the unconscious, a search for infantile traumas, the freeing of a libido that supposedly existed behind all the phenomena of the affective life, an uncovering of such mythical impulses as the death instinct—psychoanalysis has long been just this; but it is tending more and more to turn its attention to the defense mechanisms and finally to admit that the subject reproduces his history only because he responds to a present situation.   (p. 36)

Foucault cites with approval Anna Freud's *The Ego and the Mechanisms of Defense* and seeks to turn it against her father's theory of psychosexual development; he suggests that one could and should describe and treat styles of defenses as they show up in the present, not regard them as clues to internal, unconscious developments, as if these unconscious states were the real causes of the pathology.

"A style of psychological coherence must be found that authorizes the understanding of morbid phenomena without taking as its referential model stages described in the manner of biological phases" (pp. 41–42). Foucault favors "a method that owes nothing to . . . the mechanistic causality of the *Naturwissenschaften;* a method that must never turn into biographical history, with its description of successive links and its serial determinism. A method that must, on the contrary, grasp sets of elements as totalities whose elements cannot be dissociated, however dispersed in the history they may be" (pp. 44–45).

The proposal that one avoid pseudoscience by defining pathological patterns of behavior without seeking underlying causes
leads Foucault from Freud's theory of the forces underlying individual history to Binswanger's existential phenomenological psychiatry. In his 128-page introduction to Binswanger's essay on
dreams, published in 1955, Foucault describes Binswanger's approach to the study of man in Heideggerian terms: "This project
situates [this study] in opposition to all forms of psychological
positivism which think they can exhaust the meaningful content
of man in the reductionist concept of *homo natura* and at the same
time relocates it in the context of an ontological reflection which
takes for its major theme presence-to-being, existence, *Dasein*."[13]
He then gives a detailed account of the relevant concepts in *Being
and Time*. In *Mental Illness and Psychology,* however, Foucault
limits himself to describing types of pathological distortions of
reality. Therefore, to understand the approach Foucault favors,
we will have to supplement his summary with an account of the
opposing understandings of mind and reality underlying the
Freudian and the existential approaches to psychiatry.

We begin with a sketch of the Freudian understanding of the
mind and then contrast it with the existential view. In his
psychological theorizing, Freud presupposed a Cartesian conception of mind. This epistemological conception is roughly that
the mind consists of a set of ideas, analogous to images or
descriptions, that represent the outside world and may correspond or fail to correspond to what is actually out in the world. At
the culmination of this tradition Franz Brentano, who was one of
Freud's teachers, claimed that mental states such as perception,
memory, desire, and belief are all "of" something or "about"
something. Brentano held that this directedness or aboutness,
which he called "intentionality," is characteristic of the mind
and of nothing else.

Freud accepted the intentionalist conception of mind as a set
of states directed toward objects by means of representations.

However, the entire tradition from Descartes to Brentano had maintained that all intentional states must be conscious, whereas Freud learned from his work with hypnosis that not every mental representation was immediately accessible to reflection. Thus Freud was led to introduce the notion of an unconscious that, like the conscious mind, was directed toward objects by means of representations, but whose representations were not directly accessible to the conscious subject. Yet these unconscious representations are what motivate us. Unconscious instinctual impulses, according to Freud, are directed via unconscious ideas. Libidinal energy causes our behavior by cathecting a specific representation or idea of some object, which we then desire for sexual gratification.

This intentionalist conception of mind, joined with the idea that some mental contents can be unconscious, leads directly to Freud's conception of pathology and therapy. Freud accounts for pathology by hypothesizing that representations deprived of consciousness remain causally active but are not integrated into the web of conscious mental states; therefore they manifest themselves to consciousness as symptoms. Thus the epistemological account of mind, when used to account for pathology, becomes a *depth* psychology concerned with the causal powers of representations buried in the unconscious.

Corresponding to this epistemological view of mind and pathology we find an epistemological conception of the therapeutic process. In depth psychology, the basic problem is that some mental contents are unconscious and not properly integrated into the ego's overall set of representations. Therapy thus consists of helping the patient to *uncover* the hidden contents and to reintegrate them into his overall mental system.

Foucault attacks this conception of pathology and its associated therapy in *The Order of Things*.[14] There he argues that psychiatry is not only mistaken in a general way in trying to be a science of human nature but that psychoanalysis, as a child of its time, is mistaken in a particular way. Psychoanalysis seeks to be a science of a particular interpretation of human nature, viz. man.[15] Man, according to Foucault, is a recent human self-interpretation in response to the collapse of religion and metaphysics. Kant accepted the finitude of human reason and sought to make this very finitude the basis of man's positive powers: "[To make] the limits of knowledge provide a foundation for the possibility of knowing."[16] Thus man, as defined by Kant, became both the source of all meaning in the universe and a meaningless object in it. Indeed, it is precisely as a finite system of representations that he is the source of all order. According to Foucault's original and illuminating account, all the sciences of man are based on, and have to struggle with, this difficult idea.

A science of the psyche based on this notion of man will thus have a typical, convoluted form. Since he is an opaque object in the world, man's own mental content is foreign and obscure to him, yet, as source of all meaning, he is "perpetually summoned towards self-knowledge."[17] If man is to be intelligible to himself, the unthought must ultimately be accessible to thought and dominated in action, yet insofar as this unthought, in its obscurity, is precisely the condition of possibility of thought and action it can never be fully absorbed into the cogito. Thus "the modern *cogito* . . . is not so much the discovery of an evident truth as a ceaseless task constantly to be undertaken afresh."[18] Foucault calls this structure, characteristic of any science of man's mind, "the cogito and the unthought."

Freudian theory is a paradigm case. "Psychoanalysis stands as close as possible . . . to that critical function which, as we have seen, exists within all the human sciences. In setting itself the task of making the discourse of the unconscious speak through consciousness, psychoanalysis is advancing in the direction of that fundamental region in which the relations of representation and finitude come into play."[19] Freud's view of therapy as the interminable task of searching out and bringing to light the self's concealed motivations is the culmination of that structure of the sciences of man that demands that one think the unthought.

Thus in Foucault's later account, psychoanalytic theory turns out to be not just a typical (pseudo) science of *human beings* but, more specifically, an exemplary (pseudo) science of *man,* in which man's nature as finite is taken to be explained by an unthought that must be, but can never be, fully recuperated by consciousness.

Heidegger, reacting against Cartesian representationalism and its modern versions, developed an alternative model of the mind's relation to reality. This account is so radical that, strictly speaking, it does not refer to the mind at all. Rather, Heidegger prefers to speak of the way the whole human being is related to the world. Indeed, even "relation" is misleading, since it suggests the coming together of two separate entities—human beings and the world—whereas Heidegger sees mind and world as inseparable. So he is finally driven to replace the epistemological relation of subject and object with a way of being he calls "being-in-the-world," in which human-being, or *Dasein,* is a kind of space in which coping with every sort of being becomes possible.

This "ontological" view does not deny that human beings sometimes have mental representations by which their minds are directed toward objects. Rather, Heidegger and the existential phenomenologists who accept and develop his view assert that mental representations and intentionality presuppose a context in which objects can show up and make sense. This context is provided by a background understanding of what count as objects, what count as human beings, and ultimately what counts as real, on the basis of which we can direct our actions toward particular things and people. Heidegger calls this background understanding of what it means to be—which is embodied in the tools, language, and institutions of a society and in all persons growing up in that society but cannot be exhaustively represented in their minds—an "understanding of being." Hence the name *ontology.* Foucault describes his research in similar ontological terms: "It was a matter of analyzing, not behaviors or ideas, nor societies and their 'ideologies' but the *problematizations* through which being offers itself [as having to be] thought—and the *practices* on the basis of which these problematizations are formed.''[20]

A culture's understanding of being creates what Heidegger calls a "clearing" (*Lichtung*) in which entities can show up for us. Maurice Merleau-Ponty, a follower of Heidegger and one of Foucault's teachers, compares this clearing to the illumination in a room. The illumination allows us to perceive objects but is not itself an object toward which the eye can be directed. He argues that this clearing is correlated with our bodily skills and thus with the bodily stance we take toward people and things. Each person not only incorporates his culture's understanding of human beings and objects, but also his subculture's and family's variations on these social practices. Thus each person comes to have or to be his own embodied understanding of what counts as real, which is, of course, not private but is a variation on the shared public world.

Take a Foucaultian example. *Christian* practices imparted an understanding of human beings as creatures of God with deep selves containing suspect desires and memories out of reach of consciousness. These aspects of the self could be recovered partially by confession, but only God could know them exhaustively. At the same time, Christianity conveyed an understanding of things as created by God and thus full of a significance that solicited endless interpretation. This unified understanding of people and things was embodied in the culture's practices and set up the possibility of the discursive structure, the cogito and the unthought, and finally Freud's therapeutic understanding of man as a confessing self.

The ontological as opposed to the epistemological view of human being leads to an alternative account of the unconscious, of psychopathology, and of therapy. Binswanger worked out and practiced this alternative. He understood psychopathology as a distortion of the human clearing that makes it narrow and rigid. He was therefore concerned with describing the style of a patient's world. For example, as Foucault explains in his intro-

duction to Binswanger's book on dreams, he was not interested
in the symbolic meaning of the *content* of dreams but in the personal *style* of structuring space and time that dreams reveal.

Binswanger used the ontological structure of a patient's existence, rather than a causal, genetic account of intrapsychic
forces, as a framework for constructing a narrative that was intended to capture the repeated pattern of a patient's life.
Foucault explains: "It is a question of restoring, through this
understanding, both the experience that the patient has of his
illness (the way in which he experiences himself as a sick or abnormal individual) and the morbid world on which this consciousness of illness opens. . . . The understanding of the sick
consciousness and the reconstitution of its pathological world,
these are the two tasks of a phenomenology of mental illness"
(p. 46).

Binswanger's therapy consisted in helping a patient to become
aware of his way of being-in-the-world and to assume responsi-
bility for it. This in itself was supposed to produce change. But
Binswanger does not explain why it is hard for a person to see the
style of his life, nor how his therapy produces this understanding,
let alone exactly why this understanding should produce change.

Merleau-Ponty offers a more plausible existential account of
psychopathology and therapy,[21] which Foucault seems to have
integrated into his account of Binswanger. In Merleau-Ponty's
ontological view, pathology occurs when the particular way a
person relates to some people or some objects becomes his way
of relating to all people and all objects, so that it becomes the
form or style of all relationships; i.e., some aspect of the epistemological relation of a subject to other persons and objects,
which should take place *in* the clearing, becomes a dimension of
the clearing itself. Merleau-Ponty calls the shift from content to
context "generalization." Foucault uses jealousy as an example
of such generalization: "One has only to think of those jealous
individuals who justify their mistrust, their interpretations, their
delusional systematizations, by a meticulous genesis of their sus-

picions that seems to dilute their symptoms throughout their existence. . . . They see in their morbid jealousy the deepest truth, the most radical misfortune of their existence. They normalize it by referring it to the whole of their previous life" (p. 48). When this happens, the person's world or clearing becomes constricted and rigid, everything important shows up as an occasion for jealousy, and the person suffers from a lack of possibilities that he cannot understand and over which he has no control. To highlight the contrast with Freudian depth psychology, this ontological account of psychopathology as the expanding of content into context might be called *breadth* psychology.

Existential psychiatry does not seek to abstract psychic components and define their normal and abnormal functioning. " 'The validity of the phenomenological descriptions is not limited by a judgment on the normal and abnormal' " (p. 56). Rather, according to Foucault, a change in *structure* distinguishes the "morbid world" from the world of a "normal man." "[The] morbid existence is . . . marked by a very particular style of abandoning the world: by losing the significations of the world, by losing its fundamental temporality" (p. 56). That is, the patient has no open future but is stuck in a past clearing so that the same issue shows up again and again. "We should probably say that it is in this circle that the essence of pathological behavior is to be found; if the patient is ill, he is so insofar as present and past are not linked together in the form of a progressive integration. . . . In contrast with the history of the normal individual, the pathological history is marked by [a] circular monotony" (p. 41).

But even if the patient were led to recognize the constrictedness of his present clearing, he would be likely to insist that at a certain time in the past he had discovered that this is simply how things are for him, his truth, his "destiny" as Foucault puts it (p. 48). Thus the therapeutic strategy for turning the ontological back into the epistemological ultimately must undermine the patient's sense of reality. This is accomplished by working with the patient to piece together an account of how the patient's narrow version of reality developed through a series of accidental events and misunderstandings. The patient must come to realize that what he takes to be his destiny is not objective reality but his own arbitrary interpretation.

Simultaneously, the patient must be lead to see the connection between his interpretation of reality and his pain. The therapist thus tries to get the patient to see both that what he takes to be unchangeable reality is simply *his* particular and quirky story and that this understanding has a high price. Such a "genealogy" of an individual's world will tend to undermine the patient's conviction that his way of seeing things is the way things are and have to be.

None of this would work, however, if every aspect of the patient's behavior had been infected by his one-dimensional view. For then the therapeutic, genealogical reconstruction of the arbitrariness of the patient's sense of reality would be seen by the patient merely as showing the strange and idiosyncratic route he followed in arriving at his truth. Fortunately, however, this need not be his response. When a patient's world becomes totalized and one-dimensional, other ways of behaving endure from earlier days. These marginal stances, interpretations, and practices are not taken up into the one-dimensional clearing precisely because they are experienced as too fragmentary and trivial. The therapist must recover and focus these lost possibilities.

Once we see how the existential psychiatrist's description of the general structure of self-interpreting beings and its distortions can and must dispense with a scientific theory of psychic components and their normal and abnormal functioning, we are finally in a position to understand Foucault's claim that "mental pathology requires methods of analysis different from those of organic pathology and that it is only by an artifice of language that the same meaning can be attributed to 'illnesses of the body' and 'illnesses of the mind' " (p. 10). Physiology can give us "valid abstractions" that allow "causal determinations." But, "whereas the idea of organic solidarity enables one to distinguish and to unite morbid damage and adapted response, the examination of personality in mental pathology prevents such analyses" (p. 12). In short, once we see that psychiatry must study "the style, the whole historical anteriority and possible implications, of an existence" (p. 11), we see that although there can be a science of the body there can be no science of the self.

In this view, we can have true, objective theories about DNA, human reproduction, sexual arousal, and so forth, but there are no objective answers to such questions as What is human nature? Are we sexual beings?—not because we do not yet know the answers to these questions, but because they are not the sort of questions that have objective answers. What one could develop is rather (1) a description of the structure of self-interpreting beings and its variations—a philosophical anthropology—and (2) a history of the experience of madness, i.e., of the series of self-interpretations embodied in our cultural practices that determine how the most extreme variations are to be understood.[22]

This is the rationale behind Parts I and II of the *second* version of this book. The first version, however, contained no such history of the experience of madness and our practices for dealing with it. Rather, Foucault, always open to a causal account of the organism and an interpretative account of practices, adopted a Soviet account of psychopathology. He held that the existential approach could be accepted as an adequate descriptive account of pathology, then broadened by showing the origin of psychopathology in objective social contradictions, and finally, grounded scientifically by showing how the social contradications affected the brain. So when in Chapter 1 of both versions Foucault notes that "in mental pathology, the reality of the patient does not permit ... abstraction and each morbid individuality must be understood through the practices of the environment with regard to him" (p. 12) and promises to analyze in Part II "the dialectic of the relations of the individual to his environment'' (p. 13), the phrases are conveniently ambiguous. They could refer to his early Marxist social analysis or to his later Heideggerian cultural account.[23]

The ambiguity concerning which environmental conditions are necessary to explain mental pathology allows Foucault to use the same transition in his introduction to Part II in both versions: "It would be a mistake to believe that organic evolution, psychological history, or the situation of man in the world may reveal these conditions. It is in these conditions, no doubt, that the illness manifests itself, that its modalities, its forms of expression, its style, are revealed. But the roots of the pathological deviation, as such, are to be found elsewhere'' (p. 60). He continues, still on two registers, in a way that anticipates and is compatible with even his last works: "Our society does not wish to recognize itself in the ill individual whom it rejects or locks up; as it diagnoses the illness, it excludes the patient. The analyses of our psychologists and sociologists, which turn the patient into a deviant and which seek the origin of the morbid in the abnormal, are, therefore, above all a projection of cultural themes'' (p. 63).

When the ambiguity of social critique is disambiguated, however, the two versions of Part II diverge totally. In the original Chapter 5 Foucault focused on mental illness in the nineteenth century and developed an example to show how pathology was the result of a struggle over the possession of property resulting from the relationship of liberty and property established by the French revolution: "The mentally ill person, in the 19th century, is one that has lost the use of the liberties that were given him by the bourgeois revolution.[24]. . . The destiny of the sick person is from then on fixed for over a century: he is alienated."[25] In this account legal alienation, based on a struggle over property, causes psychological alienation. "Alienation is therefore, for the sick person, much more than a juridical status: a real experience, it necessarily inscribes itself in pathological fact. . . . The practices that crystalize around the notion of alienation have, in their turn, perhaps developed those symptomatic forms where the subject denounces the confiscation of his will and his thought, the influence put upon him, the feelings of strangeness that distance him from human meanings in a cold and absurd world.''[26]

In the second version this attempt to give a socioeconomic derivation of pathological symptoms was dropped and only the conclusion to Chapter 5 was preserved. It is used in the overall conclusion to *Mental Illness and Psychology.* In this conclusion Foucault plays on the ambiguity to combine a Marxian social critique and a Heideggerian cultural critique of Freud:

> If illness finds a privileged mode of expression in this interweaving of contradictory acts, it is not because the elements of the contradiction are juxtaposed, as segments of conflict, in the human unconscious, but simply because man makes of man a contradictory experience. The social relations that determine a culture, in the form of competition, exploitation, group rivalry,[27] or class struggle, offer man an experience of his human environment that is permanently haunted by contradiction.... Man has become for man the face of his own truth as well as the possibility of his death....The Oedipus complex, the nexus of familial ambivalences, is like the reduced version of this contradiction.   (p. 82)

Continuing his critique of Freud, Foucault simply substitutes, in the following paragraph, ''our culture'' for ''capitalism'' (p. 83) and replaces ''Its origin is, in reality, in the contradiction of social relations''[28] with a new last sentence. ''Our culture was experiencing at that time, in a way that was clear for itself, its own contradictions: man had to renounce the old dream of solidarity and admit that he could and must experience himself negatively, through hate and aggression. Psychologists have called this experience 'ambivalence' and have seen it as a conflict of instincts. A mythology built on so many dead myths'' (p. 83).

We have been seeing that, strictly speaking, Foucault did not simply substitute a new Part II for the old one. He retained the Introduction and modified and relocated parts of Chapter 5. He did, however, totally discard his old Chapter 6. Foucault had found in the work of Pavlov and his associates an argument that mental illness is the result of a disturbance of "the internal dialectic of excitation and inhibition."[29] So in Chapter 6 he argued that organic pathology, while not the initiating cause of mental illness, is the proximal cause, since social contradictions disrupt the normal functioning of the brain.

This account might seem to conflict directly with the idea that, due to the unity of *Dasein,* one can give only a phenomenological description of neuroses and psychoses as styles of existence, never a scientific explanation of their causes. If, however, we remember that for Binswanger and the existential therapists description was not meant to replace *all* explanation, but only *psychological* explanation, we can see that some story about the brain's role in psychopathology, whether it be Pavlov's now outmoded idea of overstrained reflexes or a more modern account of the role of neurotransmitters, could be a desirable and consistent supplement to existential psychiatry.

Foucault simply reversed the classical story. While "classical pathology readily admits that the primary fact is in the *abnormal* in a pure state; that the abnormal crystallizes around itself the pathological conducts that form the totality of the *illness;* and that the alteration of the personality which results, constitutes the alienation,"[30] in Foucault's account, social contradictions cause alienation, alienation causes defenses, defenses cause brain malfunction, and brain malfunction causes abnormal behavior. In short: "It is not because one is ill that one is alienated, but insofar as one is alienated that one is ill."[31]

In this "materialist" account, only a social revolution can cure mental illness: "Only if it is possible to change [social] conditions, will the illness disappear insofar as it is a functional disturbance resulting from the contradictions in the environment."[32] Provisionally, if not too consistently, however, Foucault suggests one can relax the brain reflexes by means of sleeping therapy—a cure popular in France at the time.[33] "Since the illness is in itself a defense, the therapeutic process must be in line with pathological mechanisms.... It is in this way that the sleeping cure acts. It reinforces the pathological inhibitions by creating a state of generalized inhibition; and, in virtue of the principle that inhibition corresponds to a process of assimilation in the nerve cell, a prolongated sleep allows functional recuperations, so that the defensive inhibitions, the centers of excitation and the pathological inertia disappear."[34]

One can see that Foucault has valiantly tried to answer the question he posed at the start: What relation can one define between mental pathology and organic pathology? One can also see why he categorically opposed republication of *Mental Illness and Personality*.

As Foucault notes in his retrospective critique, the unstable relation of philosophical anthropology and social history in *Mental Illness and Personality* lead him to start again and attempt a history of the forms of the experience of madness. This required a "nominalist reduction of philosophical anthropology" by means of "the history of societies." Foucault's next work, *Madness and Civilization*,[35] published in 1961, pursues this new approach. The new Chapters 5 and 6 of *Mental Illness and Psychology* provide a stunning ten-page summary of this 580-page work.

But Foucault was not happy with the second version, *Mental Illness and Psychology*, either, and for good reasons. The method Foucault adopts in his history of madness is an unstable synthesis of early Heidegger's existential account of *Dasein* as motivated by the attempt to cover up its nothingness and later Heidegger's historical interpretation of our culture as constituted by its lack of understanding of the role of the clearing in both making possible and limiting a rational account of reality. Thus to understand the tension in *Madness and Civilization*, reflected in the new Part II of *Mental Illness and Psychology*, one must return to Heidegger.

In *Being and Time,* Heidegger calls *Dasein's* nothingness, its lack of rational grounding for its actions, "strangeness" (*Unheimlichkeit*), and he focuses on the experience of this strangeness—anxiety. He sees everyday activity as a cover-up of this experience and hermeneutics as a mode of interpretation that requires the violent wrenching away of public disguises. "Dasein's *kind of being* thus *demands* that any ontological interpretation which sets itself the goal of exhibiting the phenomena in their primordiality, *should capture the being of the entity, in spite of this entity's own tendency to cover things up.* Existential analysis, therefore, constantly has the character of doing violence whether to the claims of everyday interpretation, or to its complacency and its tranquilized obviousness."[36]

Heidegger's method is thus an instance of what Paul Ricoeur has called the "hermeneutics of suspicion." In any such account one understands current conditions to be the result of a cover-up of the truth, e.g., the truth of the class struggle or the libido. Only some authority that has already unmasked the concealed truth (the Marxist theorist, the Freudian therapist) can force the self-deluded participants to see it too. In *Being and Time* Heidegger calls the enlightened authority, already present in each person's sense of his condition, "the voice of conscience." Furthermore, in any case where the truth is repressed, the real problem is the restrictions erected as defenses against the truth; thus facing the truth is supposed to bring about some sort of liberation. Marx promises the power released by realizing that one's class is exploited; Freud offers the control gained from recovering the repressed secrets of one's sexuality; and Heidegger claims that the realization that our guidelines for action cannot be grounded—which he calls holding onto anxiety—gives *Dasein* increased openness, flexibility, and even gaiety.

Foucault's Marxist Chapter 5 was methodologically compatible with his account of existential therapy because both were examples of the hermeneutics of suspicion. Binswanger understood mental pathology as inauthenticity—a refusal to accept human freedom, which could occur in any culture. The Marxist methodology implicitly assumed that social alienation, the cause of mental alienation, was likewise something fixed whose disguised manifestations could be traced continuously through history. So in Chapter 5 Foucault traced how the various interpretations of mental pathology from the Middle Ages to the Renaissance to the present age covered up what was really social alienation and mental illness. In the revised Chapter 5, however, Foucault rejects with disdain the idea of some unchanging underlying individual and social pathology: "It has been said, only too often, that, until the advent of a positivist medicine, the madman was regarded as someone 'possessed.' And all histories of psychiatry up to the present day have set out to show that the madman of the Middle Ages and the Renaissance was simply an unrecognized mentally ill patient" (p. 64).

Foucault had been reading later Heidegger, and later Heidegger rejects his earlier claim there is any underlying ahistorical truth about human beings, even that human beings are essentially self-concealing—that *Dasein* is dimly aware of its "nullity" and is actively engaged in trying to cover it up. For later Heidegger, what is left out is still strangeness, but his account of concealment is not motivated by flight. At a certain moment in history—in Classical Greece—Western man begins a project of the rational explanation of everything. This leads to a series of cultural practices that, in effect, progressively forget the clearing and thus the limits of human reason and control. For later Heidegger, since human beings do not necessarily *experience* strangeness, the Western concealment of man's special way of being cannot be understood as a motivated cover-up that must be violently unmasked. Rather, it is understood as a cultural interpretation with great advantages but even greater costs.

Once one sees that Western human beings at least are constituted by specific historical practices, one no longer seeks the general structure of the personality and the effects on the personality of objective social arrangements. Just as Marxist social considerations undermined Freud, so Heideggerian cultural considerations undermine Marxism. There is no universal truth about personality and mental illness to be recovered beneath a socially motivated, distorted interpretation. For Foucault, influenced by later Heidegger, it is no longer possible to speak of mental illness, personality, and psychology as if these notions had an objective reference independent of the practices that give them meaning. What counts as personality and mental illness is itself a function of historical interpretation. The task thus changes from situating personal existence in a concrete social situation to studying the historical and discursive practices that define a "psychology" in which the notion of mental illness becomes thinkable as something that can be the object of scientific study. It is not, as the title of the first edition, *Mental Illness and Personality,* suggested, a question of situating the sick *personality* in a concrete social context, but, as the second title, *Mental Illness and Psychology,* implies, of situating *psychology,* as a human science, in its historical context. The same shift is reflected in the change in title of Chapter 5 from "The Historical Meaning of Mental Alienation" to "The Historical Constitution of Mental Illness." This shift gives new meaning to a passage salvaged from the original Chapter 5 and moved to the end of the new Chapter 6:

> To sum up, it might be said that the psychological dimensions of mental illness cannot, without recourse to sophistry, be regarded as autonomous. To be sure, mental illness may be situated in relation to human genesis, in relation to individual, psychological history, in relation to the forms of existence. But, if one is to avoid resorting to such mythical explanations as the evolution of psychological structures, the theory of instincts, or an existential anthropology, one must not regard these various aspects of mental illness as ontological forms.[37]   (p. 84)

Where does this leave existential psychiatry? Had Foucault used Binswanger against Freud in the early version only to nominalize and thus reject the whole existential framework once he discovered the history of forms of experience? This would, indeed, account for why Foucault opposed translation and republication of version two, but since, on this reading, Part I and Part II would cancel each other out, it would make incomprehensible why he published the revised version in the first place. A more plausible view would be that, like later Heidegger, he continued to accept the existential account of the invariant structure of human beings as self-interpreting beings and of the way such a structure can be given various contents, but he came to see that cultures always restrict the space of human possibilities, so that any given variation might count as mad in one culture and not in another, and that only in our modern culture has madness come to be regarded as illness. It follows not that an analysis of existential structures should be rejected but that to study their "distortions" in isolation would give us a mythical account of mental disorders. He can thus retain his general account of *Dasein* and still raise the question: "Is there not in mental illness a whole nucleus of significations that belongs to the domain in which it appeared—and, to begin with, the simple fact that it is in that domain that it is circumscribed *as* an illness?" (p. 56).

But there are other problems. In the revised version Foucault remains in the grip of the early Heideggerian hermeneutics of suspicion. When Foucault traces the history of madness in the new Chapter 6, he speaks of "the night of [Western man's] truth" (p. 74), which was progressively excluded by a kind of conspiracy.[38] "Shakespeare and Cervantes, at the end of the Renaissance, attest to the great prestige of madness. . . . Up to about 1650, Western culture was strangely hospitable to these forms of experience. . . . About the middle of the seventeenth century, a sudden change took place: the world of madness was to become the world of exclusion" (p. 67).

Like early Heidegger on anxiety and strangeness, Foucault speaks of an "ambiguous experience that allows strangeness to reside at the very heart of the familiar" (p. 77), and like a historicized version of Heidegger's account of the reign of inauthentic public practices, Foucault tells us that this truth was progressively suppressed: "Madness, which had for so long been overt and unrestricted, which had for so long been present on the horizon, disappeared. It entered a phase of silence" (pp. 68–69). "Anxiety" in the face of madness was silenced by bringing madness under the double denomination of science and morality. Pathology makes science possible and science then turns and defines the pathological as the deviant. "It must not be forgotten that 'objective,' or 'positive,' or 'scientific' psychology found its historical origin and its basis in pathological experience.... Man became a 'psychologizable species' only when his relation to madness made a psychology possible, that is to say, when his relation to madness was defined by the external dimension of exclusion and punishment and by the internal dimension of moral assignation and guilt" (p. 73). Psychology "invites objective reductions (on the side of *exclusion*) and constantly solicits the recall to self (on the side of *moral assignation*)" (p. 74). These themes of punishment and objectification, along with guilt and subjectification, were elaborated in a new and convincing form in later Foucault's work on the prison and on sexuality. In *Mental Illness and Psychology,* however, Foucault's exploration of these themes was left undeveloped due to his unquestioning acceptance of the hermeneutics of suspicion, which led him to look for a connection between scientific truth-seeking and alienation—the repression of a deep, nonobjectifiable truth. "The very notion of 'mental illness' is the expression of an attempt doomed from the outset. What is called 'mental illness' is simply *alienated madness,* alienated in the psychology that it has itself made possible" (p. 76). Thus madness must be uncovered and returned to language: "Madness [must be] freed and disalienated, restored in some sense to its original language" (p. 76).

In the second version of *Mental Illness and Psychology,* Foucault it seems avoids an objective social realism only to fall into a subjective realism. He replaces a Marxist critique of the psychoanalytical account of mental illness as a cover-up of socioeconomic contradictions with an account of the constitution of mental illness as the last stage of a historical denial of the experience of strangeness. In the first version Foucault criticized a Freudian hermeneutics of suspicion using a social version of the hermeneutics of suspicion, thereby replacing Freud's science of the individual personality with Marx's science of society. Then, in the second version, he replaced the class struggle as the truth that is covered up with a historicized version of early Heidegger's claim that the truth that is covered up is strangeness, i.e., that there is no objective truth about the nature of human beings. But through it all he retains the conspiracy theory that something is being excluded because the interested parties do not want to face it. He also still holds that facing what is excluded would bring liberation. Just as for early Heidegger authentic *Dasein* becomes free by holding onto anxiety, so for Foucault madness offers the liberating possibility of facing our limit: "Hölderlin, Nerval, Roussel, and Artaud . . . hold out the promise to man that one day, perhaps, he will be able to be free of all psychology and be ready for the great tragic confrontation with madness" (pp. 74-75).

When in his next books, *The Birth of the Clinic* and *The Order of Things,* Foucault rejects hermeneutics, he is rejecting, with Freud, Marx, and early Heidegger, his own historical brand of the hermeneutics of suspicion, the claim that madness has been silenced and must be allowed to speak its truth. In *The Birth of the Clinic* Foucault opposes all hermeneutics, which he calls exegesis or commentary, as the mistaken attempt to liberate a deep truth covered up by everyday discourse. According to Foucault, commentary seeks "the reapprehension through the manifest meaning of discourse of another meaning at once secondary and primary, that is, more hidden but also more fundamental."[39] Hermeneutics thus "dooms us to an endless task . . . [because it] rests on the postulate that speech is an act of 'translation'. . . of the Word of God, ever secret, ever beyond itself." Foucault has come to think that the cover-up story is implausible and that there is no saving truth buried in our tradition. He dismisses all approaches that presuppose some hidden saving truth with the remark: "For centuries we have waited in vain for the decision of the Word."[40] Foucault explicitly applies this critique to *Madness and Civilization* in *The Archaeology of Knowledge,* where he notes: "It would certainly be a mistake to try to discover what could have been said of madness at a particular time by interrogating the being of madness itself, its secret content, its silent, self-enclosed truth."[41]

Rejecting the hermeneutic approach that reads history in terms of the exclusion and return of truth left Foucault with no way to interpret history at all. He asks in *The Archaeology of Knowledge:* "Is there not a danger that...the historico-transcendental thematic may disappear, leaving for analysis a blank, indifferent space, lacking in both interiority and promise?"[42]

For a time Foucault accepted this consequence, but he still had much to mine from Heidegger. In his change from digging out the ahistorical structure of *Dasein* to interpreting the historical constitution of Western man, Heidegger gave up the hermeneutics of suspicion and no longer thought in terms of exclusion. He also questioned the view of his student, Hans-Georg Gadamer, that there was a saving truth hidden in the Western tradition,[43] but he did not give up the attempt to make sense of our history. Rather he came to reflect on rationality, efficiency, and control and how these technological practices gradually came to encompass every aspect of our culture. For later Heidegger the history of the West is directed not by fear and exclusion but by the promise of power.[44] Later Foucault too, in *Discipline and Punish* and *The History of Sexuality,* turned to an interpretation of our historical practices as embodying a strategy without conscious or unconscious motivation.[45] The result was an analysis of the dangerous tendency of modern norms to expand to cover all aspects of behavior. Foucault held that because modern norms are supposedly grounded in science, like science they take every anomaly, every attempt to evade them, as occasions for further intervention and normalization.

In the last round of his fight with Freud, Foucault is thus in a position to support his accusation, already adumbrated in *Mental Illness and Psychology,* that psychoanalysis is not only a typical case of the hermeneutics of suspicion, but a paradigm case of normalizing confessional technology. In his lectures and interviews alluding to his as yet unpublished *Confessions of the Flesh,* Foucault argues that Christian confessional practices produced a being he calls "the man of desire." This Christian man identified himself not with his public deeds but with his most private intentions, desires, fantasies, and dreams. Moreover, since what one desired might well be forbidden and thus the desire disguised, one had to be suspicious of one's desires and constantly work to dredge up one's true motivations. Foucault quotes a confession manual: "Examine... all your thoughts, every word you speak, and all your actions. Examine even unto your dreams, to know if, once awakened, you did not give them your consent. And finally, do not think that in so sensitive and perilous a matter as this, there is anything trivial or insignificant."[46] Foucault now sees this as the motto of the hermeneutic subjects we have all become. "The West has managed not only... to annex sex to a field of rationality, which would not be all that remarkable an achievement, seeing how accustomed we are to such 'conquests' since the Greeks, but to bring us almost entirely—our bodies, our minds, our individuality, our history—under the sway of a logic of concupiscence and desire. Whenever it is a question of knowing who we are, it is this logic that henceforth serves as our master key."[47]

Freud's claim to have developed a science of the individual subject culminates this history. But later Foucault, like the Foucault of *Mental Illness and Psychology,* finds unfounded Freud's claim to have elaborated a science of the subject on the model of successful organic medicine by understanding desire as sexual desire, and sexual desire as what philosophers of science call a "natural kind" about which we can discover laws of normal functioning. "The notion of 'sex' made it possible to group together, in an artificial unity, anatomical elements, biological functions, conducts, sensations, and pleasures, and it enabled one to make use of this fictitious unity as a causal principle."[48] Moreover, later Foucault adds that the sexual human nature to which this pseudoscience appeals is a power-construction. "Causality in the subject, the unconscious of the subject, . . . the knowledge he holds unbeknown to him, all this found an opportunity to deploy itself in the discourse of sex. Not, however, by reason of some natural property inherent in sex itself, but by virtue of the tactics of power immanent in his discourse."[49]

A history of confessional practices exhibits and explains the logic of the cogito and the unthought. In classical Freudian theory, since pathology arises from repressed unsatisfied desires returning as symptoms, health would consist in constantly retrieving the repressed desires so as either to satisfy them, substitute other acceptable goals, or maturely resign oneself to not being able to fulfill one's infantile and antisocial demands. But we can never complete the task of putting our secret sexuality into words. "We convince ourselves that we have never said enough on the subject, that, through inertia or submissiveness, we conceal from ourselves the blinding evidence, and that what is essential always eludes us, so that we must always start out once again in search of it."[50]

In response to this inevitable impasse, Freudian theory advocates, at least in principle, the interminable analysis of one's desires, fantasies, and dreams and so contributes to the practices that tend to make everyone into a self-normalizing subject. Each person is led to seek the truth about himself and thus to assure that all his actions and even his thoughts in every area of life do not deviate from what science has shown to be normal, healthy, and productive. According to Foucault, this endless self-analysis, in which each subject is urged to speak so as to make himself available to inspection and correction, has become not our cure but our curse.

We have seen that, according to existential psychiatry, an individual can come, through a series of historical accidents, to have a one-dimensional, normalizing understanding of reality, in which every anomaly must finally be made to yield its truth and confirm his systematic interpretation. In a similar manner our culture, in its pursuit of objective truth and the total ordering of all beings for the sake of efficiency, health, and productivity, has reached a stage in which human beings can show up only as sexual individuals, each striving to be a normal subject so as to maximize his human potential.

Later Foucault thus rejoins the theme of Chapter 6 of *Mental Illness and Psychology*. The ultimate form of alienation in our society is not repression and exclusion of the truth but rather the constitution of the individual subject as the locus of pathology. Given our modern Western understanding of reality in all accounts of ourselves, whether they be pseudoscientific or existential, "Man has a relation with himself and inaugurates that form of alienation that turns him into *Homo psychologicus*" (p. 74). All forms of psychotherapy can at best provide only isolated and temporary "cures." As manifestations of our everyday cultural practices, all psychotherapies solve individual problems without combating our general malaise.

Just as in *Mental Illness and Psychology* psychoanalysis was seen as more misguided than existential analysis, so later Foucault still focuses his critique on Freud. The constitution of the subject as the locus of a deep truth, the demand for confession, and the claim to know scientifically grounded norms are the real danger. Foucault never denies that people's desires are important aspects of their personality and that, for example, when one's actions are self-defeating, it makes sense to seek help to find out what one really wants and whether one might be caught in some repetitive pattern. He never had reason to retract his remark at the end of *Mental Illness and Psychology:* "What has just been said is not intended as an a priori criticism of any at-

tempt to circumscribe the phenomena of madness or to define a
strategy of cure. It was intended simply to show a particular relation between psychology and madness and a disequilibrium so
fundamental that they rendered vain any attempt to treat *the
whole of madness, the essence and nature of madness, in terms
of psychology*" (p. 76; my italics). What makes Freudian theory
uniquely dangerous, according to later Foucault, is that self-
inspection is not confined to a period of therapy when dealing
with a specific problem. Instead, psychoanalysis as a science of
the psyche claims the authority to assert that, if one is to become
and remain a mature and healthy human being, relentless self-
inspection should in principle be practiced as a permanent way of
life. Freudian theory thus reinforces the collective practices that
allow norms based on alleged sciences of human nature to
permeate every aspect of our lives.

Late Foucault thus regards psychoanalysis as an especially
dangerous pseudoscience—an allegedly scientific theory of normal functioning, which justifies a therapy aiming to liberate us
from the supposed causal effects of repressed desires by requiring
us constantly to confess the truth about the contents of our
minds. Since an existential account of psychopathology is not
committed to these claims and practices, we can see why such an
account was once, and might well still be, acceptable to him.

But how can Foucault convince us of his view? Why can't we
think—indeed, as creatures of our age, are we not forced to
think?—that after a long history of false starts Freud finally
discovered that human beings have a normative nature, a nature
that is sexual through and through, just as we have learned that
the heart is a pump and the brain is not a radiator but the seat of
thought?

We have seen that Foucault could easily deny the truth of
psychoanalysis if he denied all serious truth-claims, as he often
seems to do, but that would be a Pyrrhic victory. Yet once he has
granted that some sciences can state the truth, how can he deny

truth to any would-be science except by entering a long and in-conclusive empirical debate? There is only one other way, and in his later works Foucault takes it: The existential therapist does not try to argue the patient out of his interpretation of reality, but rather starts with the patient's distress, amplifies and focuses it, and then seeks to dislodge the understanding of being that corre-lates with this distress. Similarly, Foucault does not seek to *prove* that our sexual interpretation of ourselves is at bottom a social construction—he writes genealogical histories.

The best way to see that things might be otherwise is to see that they once *were* and in some areas of life still *are* otherwise, and to see as well how we developed our present narrow view. Thus, following Nietzsche, Foucault sees his work as a genealogy, writ-ten to help us derealize, and so move beyond, the suffocating understanding of reality that has gradually emerged in the history of the West. Foucault does not think, any more than Nietzsche did, that such genealogy will provide an instant cure, enabling the genealogist to step outside himself and his culture. Historical therapy nonetheless loosens the grip of our current understand-ing of reality by letting us see how we got where we are and the cost of our current understanding. Without stepping out of history or seeking a philosophical grounding for objective truth-claims, genealogy can show us the accidental status of our sense of who we are, and it can sensitize us to practices still alive in our culture that have not been taken up into the reigning under-standing of being.

Foucault's early interest in the relation of madness and medicine never left him. Indeed, one can think of later Foucault as practicing genealogical therapy on the madness of modernity. He is trying to historicize, and so help dissolve, the closed, nor-malized view we have of ourselves as hermeneutic subjects in order to ready us for the possibility of a new interpretation of the human self that could take up currently marginalized practices, thus opening up our world rather than shutting it down.[51]

Foucault paraphrases and presumably agrees with Nietzsche when he says: "Historical sense has more in common with medicine than philosophy. ... Its task is to become a curative science."[52]

Hubert L. Dreyfus
University of California, Berkeley

NOTES

1. Michel Foucault, "Preface to *The History of Sexuality*, Volume II," trans. William Smock, in *The Foucault Reader*, ed. Paul Rabinow (New York: Pantheon Books, 1984), p. 334. Rabinow has published an early draft, which differs from the preface published in Michel Foucault, *The Use of Pleasure*, trans. Robert Hurley (New York: Vintage, 1986).

2. Michel Foucault, *Maladie Mentale et Personalité* (Paris: Presses Universitaires de France, 1954). This work was not translated into English. All translations are my own.

3. Michel Foucault, *Maladie Mentale et Psychologie* (Paris: Presses Universitaires de France, 1962); trans. by Alan Sheridan as *Mental Illness and Psychology* (New York: Harper & Row, 1976).

4. Page references to *Mental Illness and Psychology* will be included in parentheses following quotations.

5. Michel Foucault, "Final Interview," *Raritan* I (Summer 1985): 8. Interview conducted by Gilles Barbadette and first published in *Les Nouvelles*, 28 June 1984. The other major influence was, of course, Nietzsche. "I am simply Nietzschean, and I try to see, on a number of points, and to the extent that it is possible, with the aid of Nietzsche's texts ... what can be done in this or that domain" (Foucault, "Final Interview," 9). But Heidegger alone influenced early Foucault and it was through Heidegger that Foucault came to appreciate Nietzsche. "It is possible that if I had not read Heidegger, I would not have read Nietzsche. I had tried to read Nietzsche in the fifties but Nietzsche alone did not appeal to me—whereas Nietzsche and Heidegger: that was a philosophical shock!" (ibid.). Moreover, it is only in Foucault's later genealogical

works that Nietzsche's influence becomes apparent. This foreword, therefore, will only touch on Nietzsche's influence on Foucault in connection with the importance of genealogy for later Foucault.

6. The year after Foucault published *Maladie Mentale et Personalité,* he published a 128-page introduction to Ludwig Binswanger's *Le Rêve et l'Existence* (Paris: Desclée de Brouwer, 1955).

7. Martin Heidegger, *Sein und Zeit* (1927); trans. by John Macquarrie and Edward Robinson as *Being and Time* (New York: Harper & Row, 1963).

8. In keeping with the thesis of Part II that organic and mental pathology only fit together in a concrete social setting, Part I in the first version ends with the phrase "It is the actual man which sustains their factual unity." As we shall see, Foucault believed in 1954 that Pavlovian theory explained the common basis of organic and mental disorders. Thus in the first version he promises to "restore the whole of the causal system which founds them" (*Maladie Mentale et Personalité,* p. 17). In the 1962 version this has been replaced by the attempt to "determine the conditions that have made possible this strange status of madness, a mental illness that cannot be reduced to any illness" (p. 13).

9. Michel Foucault, "La Vie: L'Expérience et la Science," *Revue de Métaphysique et de Morale,* 1, 6–14 (1985): 3.

10. Michel Foucault, *The Archaeology of Knowledge,* trans. A. M. Sheridan-Smith (New York: Harper & Row, 1976), p. 188.

11. Michel Foucault, *Discipline and Punish: The Birth of the Prison,* trans. Alan Sheridan (New York: Pantheon, 1977), p. 226.

12. Heidegger, *Being and Time,* Sections 43 and 69. For an elaboration of this nonstandard interpretation of Heidegger, see H. Dreyfus, *Being-in-the-World: A Commentary on Division I of "Being and Time,"* (Cambridge: MIT Press, forthcoming).

13. Foucault, Introduction to Binswanger, *Le Rêve et l'Existence,* p. 10.

14. Michel Foucault, *The Order of Things* (New York: Vintage, 1973).

15. For Heidegger's critique of humanism, see "The Age of the World Picture," in *The Question Concerning Technology,* trans. William Lovitt (New York: Harper & Row, 1977); originally published in his book *Holzwege* (1952).

16. Foucault, *The Order of Things,* p. 317.

17. Ibid., p. 323.

18. Ibid., p. 324.

19. Ibid., p. 374.

20. Foucault, *The Use of Pleasure,* p. 11. Brackets indicate where I have made the translation more literal.

21. Maurice Merleau-Ponty, *Phenomenology of Perception* (London: Routledge and Kegan Paul, 1962), pp. 158ff.

22. One could, presumably, also work out a history and typography of the extreme variations themselves, as long as one were clear that this was not an objective science.

23. For a detailed comparison of the two texts, to which my account is indebted, see Pierre Machery, "Aux Sources de *l'Histoire de la Folie:* Une Rectification et Ses Limites," *Critique* 42 (August–September 1986): 753–774.

24. Foucault, *Maladie Mentale et Personalité,* p. 80.

25. Ibid., p. 81.

26. Ibid., p. 82.

27. In the second version "group rivalry" replaces "imperialist wars."

28. Foucault, *Maladie Mentale et Personalité,* p. 87.

29. Ibid., p. 93.

30. Ibid., p. 103.

31. Ibid.

32. Ibid., p. 107.

33. Ibid., p. 108.

34. Ibid.

35. Michel Foucault, *Histoire de la Folie à l'Age Classique* (Paris: Librairie Plon, 1961); *Madness and Civilization,* trans. Richard Howard (New York: Pantheon Books, 1965).

36. Heidegger, *Being and Time,* p. 359.

37. Foucault omits "one must not confuse the diverse aspects of the disease with its actual origins" *(Maladie Mentale et Personalité,* p. 89).

38. The word "conspiracy" is actually used in *Madness and Civilization,* p. ix.

39. Foucault, *The Order of Things,* p. 373.

40. Michel Foucault, *The Birth of the Clinic* (New York: Vintage Books, 1975), p. xvi.

41. Foucault, *The Archaeology of Knowledge,* p. 32.

42. Ibid., p. 39.

43. For Gadamer's version of hermeneutics, see Hans-Georg Gadamer, *Truth and Method* (New York: The Seabury Press, 1975).

44. See Heidegger's "The Question Concerning Technology," in *The Question Concerning Technology,* trans. William Lovitt (New York: Harper & Row, 1977); originally published in *Vorträge und Aufsätze* (1954).

45. Foucault, *History of Sexuality,* Vol. 1: *An Introduction,* trans. Robert Hurley (New York: Random House, 1978), p. 95.

46. Ibid., p. 20.

47. Ibid., p. 78.

48. Ibid., p. 154.

49. Ibid., p. 70.

50. Ibid., p. 33.

51. For a detailed account of Foucault's genealogical method, see Dreyfus and Rabinow, *Michel Foucault: Beyond Structuralism and Hermeneutics,* 2nd ed. (Chicago: University of Chicago Press, 1982).

52. Michel Foucault, "Nietzsche, Genealogy, and History," in *Michel Foucault: Language, Counter-Memory, Practice: Selected Essays and Interviews,* ed. D. F. Bouchard (Cornell University Press, 1977), p. 156.

Introduction

Two questions present themselves: Under what conditions can one speak of illness in the psychological domain? What relations can one define between the facts of mental pathology and those of organic pathology? All psychopathologies are ordered according to these two problems: there are the psychologies of heterogeneity, which refuse, as Blondel has done, to read the structures of morbid consciousness in terms of normal psychology; on the other hand, there are the psychologies, psychoanalytic or phenomenological, that try to grasp the intelligibility of all, even insane, behavior in significations prior to the distinction between normal and pathological. A similar division is to be found in the great debate between psychogenesis and organogenesis: the search for an organic etiology, dating from the discovery of general paralysis, with its syphilitic etiology; and the analysis of psychological causality, on the basis of disorders having no organic basis, which was defined at the end of the nineteenth century as the hysterical syndrome.

These problems have been discussed ad nauseam, and it would be quite pointless to go over once more the debates to which they have given rise. But one might ask oneself whether our distaste does not spring from the fact that we give the same meaning to the notions of illness, symptoms, and etiology in mental pathology and in organic pathology. If it seems so difficult to define psychological illness and health, is this not because one is trying in vain to apply to them, en masse, concepts that are also intended for somatic medicine? Does not the difficulty in finding unity in organic disturbances and personality changes lie in the fact that they are presumed to possess the same type of structure? Beyond mental pathology and organic pathology, there is a general, abstract pathology that dominates them both, imposing on them, like so many prejudices, the same concepts and laying down for them, like so many postulates, the same methods. I would like to show that the root of mental pathology must be sought not in some kind of "metapathology," but in a certain relation, historically situated, of man to the madman and to the true man.

However, a brief account is called for, both to recall how the traditional or more recent psychopathologies were constituted and to indicate the a prioris that mental medicine must be aware of if it is to acquire new rigor.

1

Mental Medicine And Organic Medicine

The general pathology referred to earlier developed in two main stages.

Like organic medicine, mental medicine first tried to decipher the essence of illness in the coherent set of signs that indicate it. It constituted a *symptomatology* in which the constant, or merely frequent, correlations between a particular type of illness and a particular morbid manifestation were picked out: auditory hallucination was seen as a symptom of a particular delusional structure; mental confusion, as a sign of a particular demential form. It also constituted a *nosography* in which the actual forms of the illness were analyzed, the stages in its evolution described, and the variants that it may present reconstructed: there were acute illnesses and chronic illnesses; episodic manifestations, alternations of symptoms, and their evolution in the course of the illness were each described.

It might be useful to schematize these classical descriptions, not only by way of example, but also to determine the original meanings of the classical terms used. I shall borrow from old works published at the beginning of the present century descriptions

3

whose archaism should not allow us to forget that they represented both a culmination and a departure.

Dupré defined *hysteria* thus: "A state in which the power of imagination and suggestibility, combined with that particular synergy of body and mind that I have called psychoplasticity, culminates in the more or less voluntary simulation of pathological syndromes, in the mythoplastic organization of functional disorders that are impossible to distinguish from those of simulators."[1] This classical definition, then, defines as major symptoms of hysteria suggestibility and the appearance of such disorders as paralysis, anesthesia, and anorexia, which do not, as it happens, have an organic basis, but an exclusively psychological origin.

Psychasthenia, since Janet, is characterized by nervous exhaustion and organic stigmata (muscular asthenia, gastrointestinal disorders, headaches); mental asthenia (a tendency to tiredness, inability to make an effort, confusion when confronted by an obstacle, difficulty in relating to the real and the present: what Janet called "loss of the function of the real"); and disorders in emotivity (sadness, worry, paroxysmal anxiety).

Obsessions: "appearance of indecision, doubt, and anxiety in a habitual mental state, and of various obsession-impulses in the form of intermittent paroxysmal attacks."[2] *Phobia,* characterized by attacks of paroxysmal anxiety when confronted by particular objects (agoraphobia when confronted by open spaces), is distinguished from *obsessional neurosis,* in which the defenses that the patient erects against his anxiety (ritual precautions, propitiatory gestures) are particularly marked.

Mania and depression: Magnan called "intermittent madness" that pathological form in which two opposed syndromes—the maniacal syndrome and the depressive syndrome—are seen nevertheless to alternate at fairly long intervals. The first of these syndromes involves motor agitation, a euphoric or choleric mood, a psychic exaltation characterized by verbigeration, rapidity of the associations, and the flight of ideas. Depression, on the other hand, takes the form of motor inertia against the background of a mood of sadness, accompanied by a psychic slowing down. Sometimes found in isolation, mania and depression are generally linked in a system of regular or irregular alternation, the different forms of which were described by Gilbert-Ballet.[3]

Paranoia: against a background of emotional exaltation (pride, jealousy) and of psychological hyperactivity, a systematized, coherent delusion, without hallucination, is seen to develop, crystallizing in a pseudological unity of themes of grandeur, persecution, and revenge.

Chronic hallucinatory psychosis is also a delusional psychosis; but the delusion is not systematized to a very great degree and is often incoherent; in the end, themes of grandeur absorb all others in a puerile exaltation of the individual concerned. In the last resort, it is sustained above all by hallucinations.

Hebephrenia, the psychosis of adolescence, is defined by intellectual and motor excitation (excessive chatter, neologisms, puns; mannerisms and impulsiveness), by hallucinations and disordered delusion, the polymorphism of which is gradually impoverished.

Catatonia can be recognized by the subject's negativism (silence, refusal to eat, and what Kraepelin called "barriers against the will"), suggestibility (muscular passivity, preservation of imposed attitudes, echo responses), stereotyped reactions, and impulsive paroxysms (sudden motor discharges that seem to break through all the barriers erected by the illness).

Observing these last three pathological forms, which occur fairly early in the development of the illness and tend toward dementia, that is to say, toward the total disorganization of psychological life (the delusion dies down, hallucinations tend to give place to disconnected dreaming, and the personality sinks into incoherence), Kraepelin grouped them together under the common term *dementia praecox.*[4] This same nosographical entity was taken up by Bleuler, who extended it to include certain forms of paranoia[5] and renamed it *schizophrenia,* an illness generally

characterized by a disorder in the normal coherence of the associations—as in a breaking up (*Spaltung*) of the flow of thought
—and, on the other hand, by a breakdown of affective contact with
the environment, by an inability to enter into spontaneous com-
munication with the affective life of others (autism).

These analyses have the same conceptual structure as those of
organic pathology: here and there, the same methods were used to
divide up symptoms into pathological groups and to define large
morbid entities. But behind this single method lie two postulates,
each of which concerns the nature of illness.

The first postulate is that illness is an essence, a specific entity
that can be mapped by the symptoms that manifest it, but that is
anterior to them and, to a certain extent, independent of them; a
schizophrenic basis was described as hidden beneath the obsessional symptoms; one referred to disguised delusion and presupposed the existence of manic-depressive madness behind a manic
attack or a depressive episode.

Side by side with this "essentialist" prejudice and as if to
compensate for the abstraction that it implied, there was a naturalist postulate that saw illness in terms of botanical species; the unity
that was supposed to exist in each nosographical group behind the
polymorphism of the symptoms was like the unity of a species
defined by its permanent characteristics and diversified in its
subgroups: thus dementia praecox was like a species characterized
by the ultimate forms of its natural development and which may
present hebephrenic, catatonic, or paranoid variants.

If mental illness is defined with the same conceptual methods as
organic illness, if psychological symptoms are isolated and assem-
bled like physiological symptoms, it is above all because illness,
whether mental or organic, is regarded as a natural essence
manifested by specific symptoms. Between these two forms of
pathology, therefore, there is no real unity, but only, and by means
of these two postulates, an abstract parallelism. And the problem
of human unity and of psychosomatic totality remains entirely
open.

It was the intractability of this problem that turned pathology toward new methods and new concepts. The notion of an organic and psychological unity swept away the postulates that erected illness into a specific entity. Illness, like independent reality, tends to elusiveness, and the attempt to see it as a natural species in relation to the symptoms and as a foreign body in relation to the organism was abandoned. On the contrary, a privileged status was accorded to the overall reactions of the individual. Between the morbid process and the general functioning of the organism, the illness no longer intervened as an autonomous reality; it was now seen simply as an abstract segmentation carried out on the development [*devenir*] of the individual patient.

In the domain of organic pathology, we should remember the role now being played by hormonal regulations and their disturbances, and the importance accorded to vegetative centers like the region of the third ventricle, which governs these regulations. We know to what extent Leriche stressed the overall character of pathological processes and the need to substitute a tissular for a cellular pathology. Selyé, for his part, in describing "diseases of adaptation," showed that the essence of the pathological phenomenon should be sought in the whole set of nervous and vegetative reactions, which act as a sort of overall response on the part of the organism to attack, to "stress," from the outside world.

In mental pathology, the same privileged status was accorded the notion of psychological totality; illness was seen as an intrinsic alteration of the personality, an internal disorganization of its structures, a gradual deviation of its development; it had reality and meaning only within a structured personality. Following this direction, an attempt was made to define mental illnesses according to the scope of the personality disturbances, and psychic disorders came to be distributed into two major categories: the psychoses and the neuroses.

1. The *psychoses* were disturbances affecting the personality as a whole and involved disorder in thinking (maniacal thinking that loses direction, drains away, or glides over associations of

sounds or puns; schizophrenic thinking, which leaps across con-
nections and proceeds by fits and starts or by contrasts); a general
alteration of the affective life and of mood (a breakdown of
affective contact in schizophrenia; excessive emotional colora-
tions in mania or depression); a disturbance in conscious control,
in seeing various points of view in perspective; alterations in the
critical sense (delusional belief in paranoia, in which the system of
interpretation precedes proof of its accuracy and remains
impermeable to any discussion; the indifference of the paranoid to
the singularity of his hallucinatory experience, which, for him, is
self-evident).

2. In the *neuroses*, on the other hand, only a part of the
personality is affected, for example, the ritualism of obsessionals
with regard to a particular object or the anxiety provoked in a
phobic neurotic by a particular situation. But the flow of thought
remains structurally intact, even if it is slower in the case of
psychasthenics; affective contact survives and, in the case of
hysterics, in an exaggerated, highly susceptible form; lastly, even
when he presents obliterations of consciousness, as in the case of
the hysteric, or uncontrollable impulses, as in the case of the
obsessive, the neurotic preserves his critical lucidity with regard to
these morbid phenomena.

Among the psychoses, one usually classes paranoia and the
whole schizophrenic group, with its paranoid, hebephrenic, and
catatonic syndromes; among the neuroses, psychasthenia, hysteria, obsession, anxiety neurosis, and phobic neurosis.

The personality thus becomes the element in which the illness
develops and the criterion by which it can be judged; it is both the
reality and the measure of the illness.

In this priority given to the notion of totality one can see a return
to concrete pathology and the possibility of determining the field
of mental pathology and that of organic pathology as a single
domain. After all, is not each, in its different ways, addressed to
the same human individual in his concrete reality? And by this
establishment of the notion of totality, do they not converge both

by the identity of their methods and by the unity of their object?

The work of Goldstein might be taken as proof of this. Studying at the frontiers of mental medicine and organic medicine a neurological syndrome like aphasia, he rejected both the organic explanations in terms of a local lesion and the psychological interpretations in terms of an overall intelligence deficit. He showed that a post-traumatic cortical lesion may alter the style of an individual's responses to his environment: functional damage reduces the organism's possibilities of adaptation and eliminates from behavior the possibility of certain attitudes. When an aphasiac cannot name an object that is shown to him, whereas he can ask for it if he needs it, it is not because of a deficit (an organic or psychological suppression) that can be described as a reality in itself; it is because he is no longer capable of a certain attitude to the world, a perspective of denomination that, instead of approaching the object in order to grasp it (*greifen*), distances him in order to show it, to indicate it (*zeigen*).[6]

In any case, whether its first designations are organic or psychological, the illness concerns the overall situation of the individual in the world; instead of being a physiological *or* psychological essence, the illness is a general reaction of the individual taken in his psychological *and* physiological totality. In all these recent forms of medical analysis, therefore, one can read a single meaning: the more one regards the unity of the human being as a whole, the more the reality of an illness as a specific unity disappears and the more the description of the individual reacting to his situation in a pathological way replaces the analysis of the natural forms of the illness.

By means of the unity that it provides and the problems that it eliminates, this notion of totality is well adapted to introduce into pathology an atmosphere of conceptual euphoria. It was from this atmosphere that those who had to any extent been inspired by Goldstein wished to benefit. But, unfortunately, the euphoria was not matched by an equal rigor.

My aim, on the contrary, is to show that mental pathology requires methods of analysis different from those of organic pathology and that it is only by an artifice of language that the same meaning can be attributed to "illnesses of the body" and "illnesses of the mind." A unitary pathology using the same methods and concepts in the psychological and physiological domains is now purely mythical, even if the unity of body and mind is in the order of reality.

1. *Abstraction.* In organic pathology, the theme of a return to the patient through the illness does not preclude the strict adoption of a perspective whereby conditions and effects, overwhelming processes and singular reactions, in pathological phenomena can be isolated. Indeed, anatomy and physiology offer medicine an analysis that authorizes valid abstractions against the background of organic totality. Certainly Selyé's pathology insists, more than any other, on the solidarity of each segmentary phenomenon with the whole organism; but this does not mean that they disappear in their individuality or that they are condemned as an arbitrary abstraction. On the contrary, it is in order to make it possible to order singular phenomena in an overall coherence, to show, for example, how intestinal lesions similar to those of typhoid take their place in a set of hormonal disturbances, one essential element of which is a disorder of the cortico-surrenal functioning. The importance given in organic pathology to the notion of totality excludes neither the abstraction of isolated elements nor causal analysis; on the contrary, it makes possible a more valid abstraction and the determination of a more real causality.

Now, psychology has never been able to offer psychiatry what physiology gave to medicine: a tool of analysis that, in delimiting the disorder, makes it possible to envisage the functional relationship of this damage to the personality as a whole. The coherence of a psychological life seems, in effect, to be assured in some way other than the cohesion of an organism; the integration of its segments tends toward a unity that makes each possible, but that is compressed and gathered together in each: this is what psychologists call, in the vocabulary that they have borrowed from phenomenology, the significant unity of behavior, which contains in each element—dream, crime, gratuitous gesture, free association—the general appearance, the style, the whole historical anteriority and possible implications, of an existence. One cannot, then, make abstractions in the same way in psychology and in physiology, and the delimitation of a pathological disorder requires different methods in organic and in mental pathology.

2. *The normal and the pathological.* Medicine has seen a gradual blurring of the line separating the pathological and the normal; or rather, it has grasped more clearly that clinical pictures were not a collection of abnormal facts, of physiological "monsters," but that they were partly made up of the normal mechanisms and adaptive reactions of an organism functioning according to its norm. Hypercalciuria, which follows a fracture of the femur, is an organic response situated, as Leriche puts it, "in line with tissular possibilities": [7] it is the organism reacting in an ordered manner to pathological damage and with a view to repairing that damage. But it must not be forgotten that these considerations are based on a coherent laying out of the organism's physiological possibilities; and analysis of the normal mechanisms of illness enables us, in fact, to discern more clearly the morbid damage and, together with the organism's normal possibilities, its potentiality for cure: just as the illness is inscribed within normal physiological possibilities, the possibility of cure is written into the process of the disease.

In psychiatry, on the other hand, the notion of personality makes any distinction between normal and pathological singularly difficult. Bleuler, for example, set up as two opposed poles of mental pathology the schizophrenia group, with its breakdown of contact with reality, and the manic-depressive group, or cyclical psychoses, with their exaggeration of affective reactions. But this definition seemed to define normal as well as morbid personalities; and, following a similar direction, Kretschmer set up a bipolar characterology involving schizothymia and cyclothymia, the pathological accentuation of which would present itself as schizophrenia and "cyclophrenia." But, at the same time, the transition from normal reactions to morbid forms was not a matter of a precise analysis of the processes; it simply made possible a qualitative appreciation that opened the way to every kind of confusion. Whereas the idea of organic solidarity enables one to distinguish and to unite morbid damage and adapted response, the examination of personality in mental pathology prevents such analyses.

3. *The patient and the environment.* A third difference prevents one from treating with the same methods and analyzing with the same concepts the organic totality and the psychological personality. It is doubtful whether any illness is separable from the methods of diagnosis, the procedures of isolation, and the therapeutic tools with which medical practice surrounds it. But, independently of these practices, the notion of organic totality accentuates the individuality of the sick subject; it makes it possible to isolate him in his morbid originality and to determine the particular character of his pathological reactions.

In mental pathology, the reality of the patient does not permit such an abstraction and each morbid individuality must be understood through the practices of the environment with regard to him. The situation of internment and guardianship imposed on the madman from the end of the eighteenth century, his total dependence on medical decision, contributed no doubt to the creation, at the end of the nineteenth century, of the personality of the hysteric. Dispossessed of his or her rights by guardian and family, thrown back into what was practically a state of juridical and moral minority, deprived of freedom by the all-powerful doctor, the patient became the nexus of all social suggestions; and at the point of convergence of these practices, suggestibility was proposed as the major syndrome of hysteria. Babinski, imposing the grip of suggestion on his patient from the outside, led her to such a point of "alienation" and collapse that, speechless and motionless, she was ready to accept the efficacy of the miraculous words, "Rise and walk." And the doctor found the sign of simulation in the success of his evangelical paraphrase, since the patient, following the ironically prophetic injunction, did indeed get up and walk. But in that which the doctor denounced as illusion, he came up against the reality of his medical practice: in the patient's suggestibility he found the result of all the suggestions, all the dependences, to which the patient had been subjected. That we no longer find such miraculous cases today does not undermine the reality of Babinski's successes, but simply proves that the face of hysteria tends to disappear with the practices of suggestion that once constituted the patient's environment.

The dialectic of the relations of the individual to his environment does not operate in the same way in pathological physiology and in pathological psychology.

So one can accept at first sight neither an abstract parallel nor an extensive unity between the phenomena of mental pathology and those of organic pathology; it is impossible to transpose from one to the other the schemata of abstraction, the criteria of normality, or the definition of the individual patient. Mental pathology must shake off all the postulates of a "metapathology": the unity that such a metapathology provides between the various forms of illness is never more than factitious; that is to say, it belongs to a historical fact that is already behind us.

So, placing our credit in man himself and not in the abstractions of illness, we must analyze the specificity of mental illness, seek the concrete forms that psychology has managed to attribute to it, then determine the conditions that have made possible this strange status of madness, a mental illness that cannot be reduced to any illness.

This work tries to answer these questions in its two parts:

I. The Psychological Dimensions of Mental Illness
II. Psychopathology as a Fact of Civilization

NOTES

1. Dupré, *La constitution émotive* (1911).
2. Delmas, *La pratique psychiatrique* (1929).
3. Gilbert-Ballet, "La psychose périodique," *Journal de psychologie,* 1909-10.
4. Kraepelin, *Lehrbuch der Psychiatrie* (1889).
5. E. Bleuler, *Dementia praecox, oder Gruppe der Schizophrenien* (1911). [*Dementia Praecox, or the Group of Schizophrenias,* tr. Joseph Zinkin (New York, 1966).]
6. Goldstein, *Journal de psychologie,* 1933.
7. Leriche, *Philosophie de la chirurgie.*

PART I

The Psychological Dimensions
of Mental Illness

2

Mental Illness And Evolution

When one is confronted by a very sick patient, one's first impression is of an overall, overwhelming deficit, with no compensation; the inability of a confused subject to relate to his situation in time and space, the ruptures of continuity that constantly occur in his behavior, the impossibility of going beyond the moment in which he is immured and acceding to the universe of others or facing the past and future—all these phenomena lead one to describe his illness in terms of suppressed functions: the patient's consciousness is disoriented, obscured, reduced, fragmented. But, at the same time, this functional void is filled by a whirl of elementary reactions that seem exaggerated and made more violent by the disappearance of other forms of behavior: all the repetition compulsions are accentuated (the patient replies to questions by echoing the question; a gesture is begun, then suddenly stops halfway, and the half-completed gesture is repeated indefinitely); the internal language invades the entire expressive domain of the subject, who pursues under his breath a disconnected dialogue, without addressing anyone; then, at certain moments, intense emotional reactions occur.

Mental pathology should not be read, therefore, in the over-

ly simple text of suppressed functions: mental illness is not only a
loss of consciousness, the slumbering of this or that function, the
obnubilation of this or that faculty. In its abstract division,
nineteenth-century psychology invited this purely negative
description of mental illness; and the semiology of each was easy
enough, confining itself to describing lost aptitudes, enumerating,
in the case of amnesias, forgotten memories, and in dual personalities, detailing the syntheses that had become impossible. In
fact, mental illness effaces, but it also emphasizes; on the one
hand, it suppresses, but on the other, it accentuates; the essence of
mental illness lies not only in the void that it hollows out, but also
in the positive plenitude of the activities of replacement that fill
that void.

What dialectic will take account both of these positive facts and
of the negative phenomena of disappearance?

It can be observed from the outset that suppressed functions and
accentuated functions are not at the same level: what has disappeared is consciousness, with its complex coordinations, its intentional openings, its play of orientation in time and space, the
tension of the will that adopts and orders the compulsions. Preserved and accentuated behavior, on the other hand, is segmentary
and simple; what we are dealing with here are dissociated elements
that are freed in a style of total incoherence. The complex synthesis
of dialogue has been replaced by fragmentary monologue; the
syntax through which meaning is constituted is broken, and all that
survives is a collection of verbal elements out of which emerge
ambiguous, polymorphic, labile meanings; the spatiotemporal
coherence that is ordered in the here and now has collapsed, and all
that remains is a chaos of successive heres and isolated moments.
The positive phenomena of the illness are opposed to the negative
phenomena as the simple to the complex.

But also as the stable to the unstable. Spatiotemporal syntheses,
intersubjective behavior, voluntary intentionality, are constantly
compromised by phenomena as frequent as sleep, as diffuse as
suggestion, as customary as dream. The behavior accentuated by

the illness possesses a psychological solidity lacking in the suppressed structures. The pathological process exaggerates the most stable phenomena and suppresses only the most labile. Lastly, the pathologically accentuated functions are the most involuntary: the patient has lost all initiative, to the point that the very response induced by a question is no longer possible for him; he can merely repeat the last words of his questioner, or when he manages to perform a gesture, the initiative is immediately overwhelmed by a repetition compulsion that arrests it and stifles it. To conclude, then, let us say that the illness suppresses complex, unstable, voluntary functions by emphasizing simple, stable, compulsive functions.

But this difference in structural level is duplicated by a difference in evolutive level. The preeminence of compulsive reactions, the endlessly interrupted and disordered succession of behavior, the explosive form of emotional reactions, are characterized by an archaic level in the evolution of the individual. It is behavior of this kind that gives children's reactions their own particular style: the absence of behavior involving dialogue, the prevalence of monologues involving no interlocutors, echo repetitions deriving from a lack of understanding of the dialectic of question and answer; the plurality of spatiotemporal coordinates, which allows isolated behavior, in which space is fragmented and moments are independent—all those phenomena that are common to pathological structures and to the archaic stages of evolution designate a regressive process in the illness.

If, therefore, in a single movement, the illness produces positive and negative signs, if it both suppresses and emphasizes, it does so to the extent that, going back to the earlier phases of evolution, it eliminates recent acquisitions and rediscovers forms of behavior that have normally been surpassed. The illness is the process throughout which the web of evolution is unraveled, suppressing first, in its most benign forms, the most recent structures, then attaining, at its culmination and supreme point of gravity, the most archaic levels. The illness is not, therefore, a deficit that strikes blindly at this or that faculty; there is in the absurdity of the morbid a logic that we must know how to read; it is the same logic as operates in normal evolution. The illness is not an essence *contra natura*, it is nature itself, but in an inverted process; the natural history of the illness has merely to flow back against the current of the natural history of the healthy organism. But in this single logic, each illness will retain its own physiognomy; each nosographical entity will find its place, and its content will be defined by the point at which the work of dissociation stops; the notion of differences of essence between illnesses should be replaced by an analysis based on the degree of depth of the deterioration, and the meaning of an illness might be defined by the level at which the process of regression is stabilized.

"In every insanity," said Jackson, "there is morbid affection of more or less of the highest cerebral centres or, synonymously, of the highest level of evolution of the cerebral sub-system, or, again synonymously, of the anatomical substrata, or the physical basis, of consciousness. . . . In every insanity more or less of the highest cerebral centres is out of function, temporarily or permanently, from some pathological process. . . ."[1] Jackson's entire work tended to give right of place to evolutionism in neuro- and psycho-pathology. Since the *Croonian Lectures* (1874), it has no longer been possible to omit the regressive aspects of illness; evolution is now one of the dimensions by which one gains access to the pathological fact.

A whole side of Freud's work consists of a commentary on the evolutive forms of neurosis. The history of the libido, of its development, of its successive fixations, resembles a collection of the pathological possibilities of the individual: each type of neurosis is a return to a libidinal stage of evolution. And psychoanalysis believes that it can write a psychology of the child by carrying out a pathology of the adult.

  1. The first object to be sought by the child is food, and the first

instrument of pleasure is the mouth—the phase of buccal eroticism
during which alimentary frustrations may fixate the weaning complexes; this is also the phase of quasi-biological connection with
the mother, in which any abandonment may cause the physiological deficits analyzed by Spitz[2] or the neuroses described by Mme.
Guex as being specifically neuroses of abandonment.[3] Mme. Séchehaye has even succeeded in analyzing a young schizophrenic to
whom a fixation at these very archaic stages of development had
brought on, in adolescence, a state of hebephrenic stupor in which
the subject lived in an anxiously diffused awareness of his
famished body.

2. With teething and the development of the musculature, the
child organizes a whole system of aggressive defense that marks
the first stage of independence. But it is also the stage at which
disciplines—and in a major way, the sphincteral discipline—are
imposed on the child, thus making him aware of parental authority
in its repressive form. Ambivalence is established as a natural
dimension of affectivity: the ambivalence of food, which satisfies
only to the degree that one destroys it by the aggressive action of
biting; the ambivalence of pleasure, which is as much from excre-
tion as from introjection; the ambivalence of satisfactions that are
sometimes permitted and rewarded, sometimes forbidden and
punished. It is during this phase that what Melanie Klein calls the
"good objects" and the "bad objects" are established; but the
latent ambiguity of these objects has not yet been mastered, and the
fixation at this period described by Freud as the "anal-sadistic
stage" crystallizes the obsessional syndromes: the contradictory
syndrome of doubt, of questioning, of constantly impulsive attrac-
tion compensated by the rigor of prohibition; precautions against
oneself, always diverted, but always recommenced; the dialectic
of rigor and willingness, complicity and refusal, in which the
radical ambivalence of the desired object may be read.

3. Related to the first erotic activities, to the refinement of
reactions of equilibrium, and to the recognition of self in the
mirror, an experience of one's own body is constituted. Affectivity

then develops as a major theme the affirmation of, or demand for, corporal integrity; narcissism becomes a structure of sexuality, and one's own body a privileged sexual object. Any break in this narcissistic circuit disturbs an already delicate balance, as can be seen in the anxiety of children faced with the castration fantasies of parental threats. It is in this anxious disorder of corporeal experiences that the hysterical syndrome occurs: the duplication of the body and the constitution of an alter ego in which the subject reads as in a mirror his thoughts, his wishes, and his gestures, of which this demonic double dispossesses him in advance; the hysterical fragmentation that subtracts from the total experience of the body anesthetized or paralyzed elements; the phobic anxiety before objects whose phantasmatic threats are believed by the patient to be aimed at the integrity of his body (Freud analyzed a case of this in the phobia of a four-year-old boy whose fear of horses concealed a terror of castration).[4]

4. Finally, at the end of childhood, the "object-choice" takes place—a choice that must involve, with a heterosexual fixation, an identification with the parent of the same sex. But in opposition to this differentiation, and to the assumption of normal sexuality, are the parents' attitude and the ambivalence of infantile affectivity: at this period, it is still, in effect, fixated in a mode of jealousy, mingled with eroticism and aggressivity, for a mother who is desired but who refuses herself or at least divides her affection; and it breaks down into anxiety before a father whose triumphant rivalry arouses both hate and the amorous desire for identification. This is the celebrated Oedipus complex, in which Freud believed that he could read the enigma of man and the key to his destiny, in which one must find the most comprehensive analysis of the conflicts experienced by the child in his relations with his parents and the point at which many neuroses became fixated.

In short, every libidinal stage is a potential pathological structure. Neurosis is a spontaneous archaeology of the libido.

Janet, too, takes up the Jacksonian theme, but from a sociological angle. The fall-off in psychological energy that characterizes illness would make the complex behavior acquired in the course of social evolution impossible and reveal, like a receding tide, primitive social behavior, or even presocial reactions. A psychasthenic cannot believe in the reality of his environment; for him, such behavior is "too difficult." What is difficult behavior? Basically, behavior in which a vertical analysis reveals the superimposition of several simultaneous forms of behavior. Killing game is one form of behavior; recounting one's exploits, after the event, is another. But at the very moment one is lying in wait for one's quarry, or actually killing the animal, to tell oneself that one is killing, that one is in pursuit, that one is lying in wait, in order, later, to be able to recount one's exploits to others; to have simultaneously the real behavior of the hunt and the potential behavior of the account is a double operation, and although apparently simpler, in fact more complicated than either of the others: it is the behavior of the present, the germ of all temporal behavior, in which the present action and the consciousness that this action will have a future, that one will later be able to recount it as a past event, are superimposed upon one another, are meshed together. The difficulty of an action may be measured, therefore, by the number of elementary forms of behavior that are implied in the unity of its development.

Let us now take the form of behavior that consists in "recounting to others," a form whose potentiality is also part of behavior in the present. To recount, or more simply, to speak, or in a still more elementary fashion, to issue an order, is not a simple matter either; first, it involves a reference to an event or an order of things, or to a world to which I have no access myself but to which others may have access in my place; I have to recognize, therefore, the point of view of others and integrate it into my own; I have to double my own action (the order that I have issued) with potential behavior, that of someone else whose task it is to carry it out. Furthermore, to issue an order always presupposes the ear that will perceive it, the intelligence that will understand it, and the body that will execute it; in the action of command is implied the potentiality of being obeyed. This means that such apparently simple actions as attention to the present, the account of previous actions, speech, all involve a certain duality that is fundamentally the duality to be found in all social behavior. If the psychasthenic finds attention to the present so difficult, therefore, it is because of the social implications that in some obscure way it contains; all those actions that contain a reversal (seeing/being seen, in presence; speaking/being spoken to, in language; believing/being believed, in narration) are difficult for him because they occur in a social context. A whole social evolution was required before dialogue became a mode of interhuman relation; it was made possible only by a transition from a society immobile in its hierarchy of the moment, which authorized only the order, to a society in which equality of relations made possible and assured potential exchange, fidelity to the past, the engagement of the future, and the reciprocity of points of view. The patient who is incapable of dialogue regresses through this whole social evolution.

According to its seriousness, every illness suppresses one or other form of behavior that society in its evolution had made possible and substitutes for it archaic forms of behavior.

1. Dialogue, as the supreme form of the evolution of language, is replaced by a sort of monologue in which the subject tells himself what he is doing or in which he holds a dialogue with an imaginary interlocutor that he would be incapable of holding with a real partner, like the psychasthenic professor who could deliver his lecture only in front of a mirror. It became too "difficult" for the patient to act under the gaze of others: that is why so many subjects, whether obsessionals or psychasthenics, present, when they feel they are being observed, phenomena of emotional release, such as tics, mimicry, and myoclonias of all sorts.

2. By losing this ambiguous potentiality of dialogue and by grasping speech only by the schematic side that it presents to the speaking subject, the patient loses mastery over his symbolic

world; and the ensemble of words, signs, rituals, in short, all that is allusive and referential in the human world, is no longer integrated in a system of meaningful equivalences; words and gestures are no longer the common domain in which one's own intentions and those of others meet, but significations existing of themselves, with an overwhelming, disturbing existence; a smile is no longer the banal response to an everyday greeting, but an enigmatic event that can be reduced to none of the symbolic equivalences of politeness; on the patient's horizon, it stands out, then, as the symbol of some mystery, as the expression of some silent, menacing irony. The world of persecution arises on every side.

3. This world, which extends from delusion to hallucination, seems to belong wholly and entirely to a pathology of belief, as interhuman behavior: the social criterion of truth ("believing what others believe") is no longer valid for the patient; and into this world that the absence of others has deprived of objective solidity, it introduces a whole world of symbols, fantasies, obsessions; the world in which the other's gaze has been extinguished becomes porous to hallucination and delusion. Thus, in these pathological phenomena, the patient is sent back to archaic forms of belief, to a state in which primitive man had not yet found the criterion of truth in his solidarity with others, in which he projected his desires and fears in phantasmagorias that weave into reality the indissociable threads of dream, apparition, and myth.

On the horizon of all these analyses there are, no doubt, explanatory themes that are themselves situated on the frontiers of myth: the myth, to begin with, of a certain psychological substance (Freud's "libido," Janet's "psychic force"), which is seen as the raw material of evolution and which, progressing in the course of individual and social development, is subject to relapses and can fall back, through illness, to an earlier state; the myth, too, of an identity between the mentally ill person, the primitive, and the child—a myth in which consciousness, shocked by the sight of mental illness, finds reassurance and is reinforced in the enveloping prejudices of its own culture. Of these two myths, the first, because it is scientific, was quickly abandoned (from Janet we have kept the analysis of behavior and not interpretation by psychological force; psychoanalysts increasingly reject the biopsychological notion of libido); the other, on the contrary, because it is ethical, because it justifies rather than explains, is still with us. Yet there is little sense in restoring an identity between the morbid personality of the mental patient and the normal personality of the child or the primitive. One has a choice, in fact, of one or the other:

—Either one more or less accepts Jackson's interpretation: "... I shall imagine that the highest cerebral centres are in four layers, A, B, C, D. ..." The first form of madness, the most benign, will be $-A + B + C + D$. "In fact, the whole person is now $B + C + D$. The term $-A$ is only given to indicate how the new person . . . differs from the earlier one. . . ." [5] Pathological regression, then, is simply a subtractive operation; but what is subtracted in this arithmetic is precisely the final term, the one that gives movement to and completes the personality; that is, "the remainder" is not an earlier personality, but a suppressed personality. How, from this fact, can the ill subject be identified with the "earlier" personalities of the primitive or the child?

—Or we extend Jacksonism and accept a reorganization of the personality; regression is not content to suppress and to free, it orders and places; as Monakow and Mourgue said of neurological dissolution:

Disintegration is not the exact inversion of integration. . . . It would be absurd to say that hemiplegia is a return to a primitive stage in the apprenticeship of locomotion. . . . Autoregulation is at work here in such a way that the notion of pure disintegration does not exist. This ideal process is masked by the organism's constantly active creative tendency to reestablish a disturbed equilibrium. [6]

There can be no question, then, of archaic personalities; we must accept the specificity of the morbid personality; the pathological structure of the psyche is not a return to origins; it is strictly original.

It is not a question of invalidating the analyses of pathological regression; all that is required is to free them of the myths that neither Janet nor Freud succeeded in separating from them. It would probably be quite useless to say, from an explanatory point of view, that, in becoming mentally ill, man becomes a child again; but, from a descriptive point of view, it is true to say that the patient manifests in his morbid personality segmentary forms of behavior similar to those of an earlier age or another culture; the illness uncovers and stresses forms of behavior that are normally integrated. Regression, therefore, must be taken as only one of the descriptive aspects of mental illness.

A structural description of mental illness, therefore, would have to analyze the positive and negative signs for each syndrome, that is to say, detail the suppressed structures and the disengaged structures. This would not involve explaining pathological structures, but simply placing them in a perspective that would make the facts of individual or social regression observed by Freud and Janet coherent and comprehensible. The outlines of such a description might be summarized as follows:

1. Disequilibrium and the neuroses are only the first degree of dissolution of the psychic functions; the damage is only to the general equilibrium of the psychological personality, and this often momentary rupture frees only the affective complexes, the unconscious emotional schemata, that have formed in the course of individual evolution.

2. In paranoia, the general disorder of mood frees an emotional structure that is merely an exaggeration of the usual behavior of the personality; but there is as yet no damage to the lucidity, the order, or the cohesion of the mental basis.

3. But, with the dream states, we reach a level at which the structures of the consciousness are already dissociated; percep-

tual control and the coherence of reasoning have disappeared; and, in this fragmentation of the conscious sphere, we witness the infiltration of dream structures that are normally freed only in sleep. Illusions, hallucinations, false recognitions, manifest in the waking state the disinhibition of forms of dream consciousness.

4. In the manic and melancholic states, dissociation reaches the instinctive-affective sphere; the emotional puerility of the manic subject, and the loss, in the case of the melancholic, of awareness of the body and of behavior of conservation, represent the negative side. The positive forms of mental illness appear in those paroxysms of motor agitation or emotional outbursts in which the melancholic subject affirms his despair and the manic subject his euphoric agitation.

5. Lastly, in confusional and schizophrenic states, the deterioration takes the form of a deficit in capacity; in a horizon in which the spatial and temporal markers have become too imprecise to facilitate orientation, thinking has disintegrated and proceeds in isolated fragments, dividing up an empty, dark world with "psychic syncopes," or is enclosed in the silence of a body whose very motility is locked up by catatonia. All that still emerges, as positive signs, are stereotypes, hallucinations, verbal schemata crystallized in incoherent syllables, and sudden affective interruptions crossing the demential inertia like meteors.

6. And it is with dementia that the cycle of this pathological dissolution closes—dementia, in which all the negative signs of the deficits flourish and in which the dissolution has become so deep that it no longer has any area to disinhibit; there is no longer a personality, only a living being.

But an analysis of this type cannot exhaust the totality of the pathological fact. It is inadequate to do so, and for two reasons:

1. It ignores the organization of morbid personalities in

which regressive structures are uncovered; however deep the dissolution may be (with the single exception of dementia), the personality can never completely disappear; what the regression of the personality rediscovers are not dispersed elements (for they never have been dispersed) or more archaic personalities (for there is no way back in the development of the personality, but only in the succession of behavioral forms). Inferior and simple as they may be, one must not omit the organizations by which a schizophrenic structures his world: the fragmented world that he describes accords with his dispersed consciousness, the time without future or past in which he lives reflects his inability to project himself into a future or to recognize himself in a past; but this chaos finds its point of coherence in the patient's personal structure, which guarantees the experienced unity of his consciousness and horizon. Thus, ill as a patient may be, this point of coherence cannot but exist. The science of mental pathology cannot but be the science of the sick personality.

2. The regressive analysis describes the orientation of the illness without revealing its point of origin. If it were no more than regression, mental illness would be like a potentiality laid down in each individual by the very movement of his evolution; madness would be no more than a possibility, the ever claimable ransom of human development. But why this or that person is ill, and is ill at this or that moment, why his obsessions have this or that theme, why his delusion involves these demands rather than others, or why his hallucinations are riveted to these visual forms rather than others, the abstract notion of regression is unable to explain. From the point of view of evolution, illness has no other status than that of a general potentiality. The causality that makes it necessary is not yet disengaged, no more than that which gives each clinical picture its particular coloring. This necessity, with its individual forms, is to be found not in an always specific development, but in the patient's personal history.

The analysis must be carried further therefore; and this evolutive, potential, and structural dimension of mental illness must be completed by the analysis of the dimension that makes it necessary, significative, and historical.

NOTES

1. "The Factors of Insanities," *Selected Writings of John Hughlings Jackson,* vol. II, p. 411.

2. Spitz, "Hospitalism," *The Psychoanalytic Study of the Child,* vols. I and II (1945, 1946).

3. G. Guex, *Les névroses d'abandon.*

4. "Analysis of a Phobia in a Five-Year-Old-Boy," *The Standard Edition of the Complete Psychological Works of Sigmund Freud,* vol. X.

5. Jackson, "The Factors of Insanities," pp. 413, 416.

6. Monakow and Mourgue, *Introduction biologique à l'étude de la neurologie et de la psychopathologie,* p. 178.

3

Mental Illness and Individual History

Psychological evolution integrates the past in the present in a unity without conflict, in an ordered unity that is defined as a hierachy of structures, in a solid unity that only a pathological regression can compromise. Psychological history, on the other hand, ignores such a simultaneity of the anterior and the present; it situates them in relation to one another by putting between them the distance that normally makes possible tension, conflict, and contradiction. In psychological evolution, it is the past that promotes the present and makes it possible; in psychological history, it is the present that detaches itself from the past, conferring meaning upon it, making it intelligible. Psychological development [*devenir*] is both evolution and history; psychic time must be analyzed both in terms of the anterior and the actual—that is, in evolutive terms—and in terms of the past and the present—that is, in historical terms. When, at the end of the nineteenth century, after Darwin and Spencer, one was astonished to discover the truth of man in his development as a living being, it was thought possible to write history in evolutionary terms, and even to subsume the first under the second: indeed, the same sophism is to be found in the sociology of the same period. The original error of psychoanalysis and, following it, of most genetic psychologies is no doubt that of failing to seize these two irreducible dimensions of evolution and history in the unity of psychological development.[1] But Freud's stroke of genius lay in being able, so early on, to go beyond the evolutionist horizon defined by the notion of libido and reach the historical dimension of the human psyche.

In psychoanalysis, indeed, it is always possible to separate that which pertains to a psychology of evolution (as in *Three Essays on the Theory of Sexuality*) and that which belongs to a psychology of individual history (as in *Five Psychoanalyses* and the accompanying texts). I spoke earlier of the evolution of affective structures as they are detailed in the psychoanalytic tradition. I should now like to borrow from the other side of psychoanalysis in order to define what mental illness is from the point of view of individual history.

Here is a case mentioned by Freud in the *Introductory Lectures on Psycho-Analysis* :[2] A woman of about fifty suspects her husband of infidelity with his secretary. An ordinary enough situation. Yet there are some very odd aspects to the case: the wife's jealousy was aroused by an anonymous letter; the author of the letter is known; it is also known that its author was motivated solely by a desire for revenge and that the allegations are factually incorrect; the wife knows all this, readily recognizes the injustice of her reproaches to her husband, and speaks quite spontaneously of the love that he has always shown her. And yet she is unable to shake off her jealousy; the more the facts proclaim her husband's fidelity, the more her suspicions are reinforced; paradoxically, her jealousy has crystallized around the certainty that her husband is not being unfaithful. Whereas, in its classical form of paranoia, jealousy is an impenetrable conviction that seeks its justification in the most extreme forms of reasoning, the case cited by Freud is an example of an impulsive jealousy that constantly questions its own basis in fact, that constantly attempts to deny itself and to be experienced in terms of remorse; it is a very curious (and relatively rare) case of obsessional jealousy.

In analysis, it emerged that this woman was infatuated with her son-in-law, but her feelings of guilt were such that she was unable to bear this wish and transferred to her husband the sin of loving someone much younger than oneself. Indeed, a deeper investigation showed that this attachment to the son-in-law was itself ambivalent and that it concealed an element of jealous hostility in which the object of rivalry was the patient's daughter: at the heart of the morbid phenomenon, then, was a homosexual fixation on the daughter.

Metamorphoses, symbolisms, transformation of feelings into their opposite, disguising of persons, transference of guilt, the redirection of remorse into accusation—what we have here is a collection of processes that contradict one another like the elements in a child's "storytelling." One might easily compare this jealous projection with the projection described by M. Wallon in *Les origines du caractère chez l'enfant*:[3] he quotes from Elsa Köhler the example of a three-year-old girl who struck her playmate and, bursting into tears, ran to her governess for consolation for being struck. One finds in this child the same structures of behavior as in the obsessional discussed above: the indifferentiation of self-awareness prevents the distinction between acting and being acted upon (striking/being struck, being unfaithful/being the victim of infidelity); furthermore, the ambivalence of feelings makes possible a sort of reversibility of aggression and guilt. In each case, one finds the same features of psychological archaism: fluidity of affective behavior, lability of personal structure in the I/others opposition. But this is not an attempt to confirm yet again the regressive aspect of mental illness.

The important thing here is that in the case of Freud's patient this regression has a very precise meaning: it was a means of escaping from a feeling of guilt; the patient escaped from her remorse at loving her daughter too much by forcing herself to love her son-in-law; and she escaped from the guilt aroused by this new attachment by transferring to her husband, by a sort of mirror projection, a love parallel to her own. The child's procedures of metamorphosing the real have, therefore, a use: they constitute a flight, an economical way of acting on reality, a mythical mode of transforming oneself and others. Regression is not a natural falling back into the past; it is an intentional flight from the present. A recourse rather than a return. But one can escape the present only by putting something else in its place; and the past that breaks through in pathological behavior is not the native ground to which one returns as to a lost country, but the factitious, imaginary past of substitutions.

—Sometimes this involves a substitution of forms of behavior: adult behavior, developed and adapted, gives place to infantile, simple, nonadapted behavior—as in the case of Janet's famous patient: at the idea that her father might fall ill, she manifested the paroxysmal forms of infantile emotion (cries, motor explosion, falling), because she refused the adapted behavior that would involve looking after him, finding the means for a slow cure, and organizing for herself an existence as a nurse.

—Sometimes a substitution of the objects themselves: for the living forms of reality the subject substitutes the imaginary themes of his earliest fantasies; and the world seems to open itself up to archaic objects, real persons fade before parental fantasies—as in the case of those phobics who, at the threshold of every act, come up against the same threatening fears; the mutilating figure of the father or the imprisoning mother stands out behind the sterotyped image of the terrifying animal, behind the vague background of anxiety that submerges consciousness.

This whole interplay of transformations and repetitions shows that, for the mentally ill, the past is invoked only as a substitute for the present situation and that it is realized only to the extent that it involves a derealization of the present.

But what is to be gained by repeating an anxiety attack? What is the sense of returning to the terrifying fantasies of childhood, of substituting the major disorders of a still inadequately regulated affectivity for the present forms of activity? Why flee the present, if only to return to unadapted types of behavior?

A pathological inertia in behavior? The manifestation of a repetition principle that Freud extrapolates into the biological reality of a paradoxical "death instinct," which tends toward the immobilized, the identical, the monotonous, the inorganic, just as the life instinct tends toward the constantly shifting mobility of organic hierarchies? This, no doubt, is to give to the facts a name that, in uniting them, rejects any form of explanation. But, in Freud's work and in psychoanalysis, other explanations can be found for this derealization of the present than the mere repetition of the past.

Freud himself had the opportunity of analyzing a symptom in process of formation. It was the case of a four-year-old boy, Little Hans, who had a phobic fear of horses.[4] It was an ambiguous fear, for he seized every opportunity of seeing horses and would run to the window whenever he heard a coach pass; but, as soon as he glimpsed the horse that he had come to see, he would yell out in terror. This fear was also paradoxical in that, at one and the same time, he feared that the horse might bite him and that the animal might stumble and kill himself. Did he or did he not wish to see horses? Was he afraid for himself or for them? Probably both. Analysis revealed that the child was at the nodal point of all the Oedipal situations: his father was determined to prevent too strong a fixation on the mother, but the attachment to the mother merely became more violent as a result, still further exasperated by the birth of a younger sister; so the father had always been an obstacle for Hans between his mother and him. It was at this point that the syndrome began to form. The most elementary symbolism of the dream material made it possible to see in the image of the horse a substitute for the paternal "imago"; and in the ambiguity of the child's fears, it is easy enough to recognize a wish for the father's death. In an immediate way, the morbid symptom is the satisfaction of a wish: the child experienced the death that he was unaware of wishing on the father in the imaginary form of the death of a horse.

But this symbolism—and this is the important point—not only is the mythical, figured expression of reality; it also plays a functional role in relation to this reality. The fear of being bitten by the horse is no doubt an expression of the fear of castration: it symbolizes the paternal prohibition of all sexual activities. This fear of being wounded is doubled by the fear that the horse itself might stumble, injure itself, and die: as if the child were defending himself from his own fear through the wish to see his father die and thus overthrow the obstacle that separated him from his mother. This wish to kill does not appear immediately as such in the phobic fantasy, it is present only in the disguised form of a fear: the child fears the death of the horse as much as his own wound. He defends himself against his death wish and rejects his own guilt in the matter by experiencing it as a fear that is equivalent to the fear he feels for himself; he fears for his father what he fears for himself; but his father has to fear only what the child is afraid to wish against him. It can be seen, then, that the expressive value of the syndrome is not immediate, but that it is constituted through a series of defense mechanisms. Two of these mechanisms have come into play in this case of phobia: the first transformed the fear for oneself into a wish to kill the person who arouses the fear; the second has transformed this wish into a fear of seeing it realized.

On the basis of this example, it can be said therefore that the advantage gained by the patient in derealizing his present in illness is originally a need to defend himself against this present. The illness has for content the whole set of reactions of flight and of defense in which he finds himself; and it is on the basis of this present, this present situation, that one must understand and give meaning to the evolutive regressions that emerge in pathological behavior; regression is not only a potentiality of evolution, it is a consequence of history.

This notion of psychological defense is of major importance. The whole of psychoanalysis has centered around it. An investigation of the unconscious, a search for infantile traumas, the freeing of a libido that supposedly existed behind all the phenomena of the affective life, an uncovering of such mythical impulses as the death instinct—psychoanalysis has long been just this; but it is tending more and more to turn its attention to the defense mechanisms and finally to admit that the subject reproduces his history only because he responds to a present situation. Anna Freud has compiled a list of these defense mechanisms: apart from sublimation, which is regarded as normal, she finds nine procedures whereby the patient defends himself and which in combination define the different types of neurosis: repression, regression, reaction formation, isolation, undoing, projection, introjection, turning against the self, and reversal.[5]

The hysteric makes use above all of repression. He subtracts from the conscious all sexual representations; as a protective measure he breaks psychological continuity, and in these "psychic syncopes" appear the unconsciousness, the obliviousness, the indifference, that constitute the hysteric's apparent "good humor"; he also breaks the unity of the body in order to efface all the symbols and substitutes of sexuality: hence the anesthesias and pithiatic paralyses.

The obsessional neurotic, on the other hand, defends himself mainly through "isolation." He separates conflictual emotion from its context; he invests it with symbols and expressions that have no apparent connection with its real content; and the forces in conflict suddenly emerge in impulsive, rigid, and absurd behavior in the midst of adapted behavior. A case of this is Freud's patient who, without knowing why, quite unable to justify her action to herself by any feeling of prudence or meanness, could not stop herself noting down the numbers of every bank note that came into her hands.[6] But this behavior, absurd in isolation, had a meaning if seen in its affective context: it echoed a wish the patient had experienced of assuring herself of a man's love by giving him a coin by way of a pledge; but all coins are similar; if, however, she had given him a bank note, which could be recognized by its number . . . And she defended herself against a love that she regarded as guilty by isolating the behavior from its affective justifications.

The paranoiac, at once persecuted and persecuting, denouncing in others' hearts his own wishes and hates, loving what he wishes to destroy, identifying himself with what he hates, is characterized above all by mechanisms of projection, introjection, and turning against the self. It was Freud who first showed that all these processes were present in paranoiac jealousy.[7] When the paranoiac reproaches his partner with infidelity, when he systematizes a whole set of interpretations around this infidelity, he simply reproaches the other with that with which he reproaches himself; if he accuses his mistress of infidelity with a friend, it is because he himself experiences precisely this wish; and he defends himself against this homosexual desire by transforming it into a heterosexual relationship and by projecting it onto the other in the form of an accusation of infidelity. But by means of a symmetrical projection, which also has the meaning of a justification and a catharsis, he will accuse of a homosexual wish the very person he himself desires, and by a reversal of the affect he will boast of a mythical hate that justifies in his eyes the attentions of his rival. It is not I who am unfaithful to you, but you who are unfaithful to me; it is not I who love him, but he who loves me and pursues me; what I feel for him is not love, but hate: such are the mechanisms by which a paranoiac, defending himself against his homosexuality, constitutes a delusion of jealousy.

The pathological reiteration of the past does have a meaning therefore; what drives it is not some "death instinct"; regression is one of these defense mechanisms, or rather it is a recourse to the sets of protective measures already established. The reiterative form of the pathological is only secondary in relation to its defensive signification.

There remains the nodal problem: what is the patient defending himself against when, as a child, he sets up forms of protection that he will reveal once more in the neurotic repetitions of his adult life? What is this permanent danger that appeared at the dawn of his psychological life, that will constantly stand out against his world, and that threatens with the ever changing faces of a danger which has remained identical?

Here again the analysis of a symptom may provide us with a guiding thread. A ten-year-old girl steals something: she takes a bar of chocolate under the eyes of the store assistant, who reprimands her and threatens to tell the girl's mother.[8] The impulsive, unadapted form of the theft immediately reveals it as neurotic. The subject's history shows quite clearly that this symptom was at the point of convergence of two forms of behavior: the wish to recover maternal affection that was being refused her, the symbol of which was here, as so often, the alimentary object; and, on the other hand, the whole set of guilt reactions that followed the aggressive effort to gain this affection. The symptom will appear as a compromise between these two forms of behavior; a child will give free rein to his need for affection by committing a theft, but he will free his tendencies to feel guilt by committing it in such a way that he will be found out. The behavior of the clumsy theft reveals itself to be in fact a very skillful act; its clumsiness is strategic: as a compromise between two contradictory tendencies, it is a way of mastering a conflict. The pathological mechanism is therefore a protection against a conflict, a defense in face of the contradiction that arouses it.

But not every conflict elicits a morbid reaction, and the tension it arouses is not necessarily pathological; it may even be the web of all psychological life. The conflict revealed by the neurotic compromise is not simply an external contradiction in the objective situation, but an immanent contradiction, in which the terms intermingle in such a way that the compromise, far from being a solution, is in the last resort a deepening of the conflict. When a child steals in order to recover lost affection and calms his scruples by allowing himself to be found out, it is clear that the result of his act will, by leading to the desired punishment, deprive him still more of the affection he lacks, increase in him the wish to win back affection that his theft symbolizes and temporarily satisfies, and thus increase the feelings of guilt. The experience of frustration and guilt reaction are thus linked, not as two divergent forms of conduct that share the behavior, but as the contradictory unity that defines the double polarity of one and the same act. Pathological contradiction is not normal conflict: normal conflict tears apart the subject's affective life from the outside; it arouses in him opposed forms of conduct; it disturbs his stability; it causes actions, then leads to remorse; it may even raise contradiction to the level of incoherence. But normal incoherence is, strictly speaking, different from pathological absurdity, which is animated from the inside by contradiction; the coherence of the jealous husband trying to convince his wife of infidelity is perfect, as is the coherence of the obsessional neurotic in the precautions he takes. But this coherence is absurd because it deepens, as it develops, the contradiction that it tries to overcome. When one of Freud's patients, with obsessional thoroughness, removed from her room every clock or watch whose ticking might disturb her sleep, she was at the same time defending herself against her sexual desires and satisfying them mythically: she removed all the symbols of sexuality, but also of the physiological regularity that the motherhood that she desired might disturb. As she satisfied her desires in a magical mode, she actually increased her feelings of guilt.[9] Where the normal individual experiences contradiction, the ill person undergoes a contradictory experience; the experience of the first opens onto contradiction, that of the second closes itself against it. In other words: normal conflict, or ambiguity of the situation; pathological conflict, or ambivalence of experience.[10]

Just as fear is a reaction to external danger, anxiety is the affective dimension of this internal contradiction. It is a total disorganization of the affective life, the major expression of ambivalence, the form in which that ambivalence is fulfilled; it is the vertiginous experience of simultaneous contradiction, the experience of a simultaneous wish for life and death, love and hate, the experiential apotheosis of psychological contradiction: the anxiety of the child who discovers through biting that the eroticism of absorption is charged with destructive aggressivity, or the anxiety of the melancholic, who, in order to snatch the loved object from death, identifies with him, becomes what he has been, but ends by experiencing himself in the death of the other and can retain the other in his own life only by rejoining him in death. With anxiety we are at the heart of pathological significations. Beneath all the protection mechanisms that particularize the illness, anxiety reveals itself and each type of illness defines a specific way of reacting to it: the hysteric represses his anxiety, obliterates it by embodying it in a physical symptom; the obsessional neurotic ritualizes, around a symbol, actions that enable him to satisfy both sides of his ambivalence; while the paranoiac justifies himself mythically by attributing to others by projection all the feelings that bear within them their own contradiction—he distributes among others the elements of his ambivalence and masks his anxiety beneath the forms of his aggressivity. It is anxiety, too, as a psychological experience of internal contradiction, that serves as a common denominator and that gives a single signification to the psychological development of an individual: it is first experienced in the contradictions of childhood and in the ambivalence that they give rise to; and under its latent thrust the defense mechanisms are erected, repeating through the whole of a lifetime their rituals, their precautions, their rigid maneuvers, whenever there is any threat of anxiety reappearing.

In a sense, it might be said, then, that it is through anxiety that psychological evolution is transformed into individual history; it is anxiety, in effect, that, by uniting past and present, situates them in relation to one another and confers on them a community of meanings. Pathological behavior seems to possess, paradoxically, an archaic content and a significative insertion in the present; this is because the present, on the point of arousing ambivalence and anxiety, brings neurotic protection into play; but this threatening anxiety and the mechanisms that set it aside have for long been fixed in the subject's history. The illness then proceeds like a vicious circle: the patient protects himself by his present defense mechanisms against a past whose secret presence arouses anxiety; but, on the other hand, against the possibility of a present anxiety, the subject protects himself by appealing to protections that were set up in earlier, similar situations. Does the patient defend himself with his present against his past, or does he protect himself from his present with the help of a history that now belongs to the past? We should probably say that it is in this circle that the essence of pathological behavior is to be found; if the patient is ill, he is so insofar as present and past are not linked together in the form of a progressive integration. Every individual, of course, has experienced anxiety and taken defensive measures against it; but the sick patient experiences his anxiety and his defense mechanisms in a circularity that makes him defend himself against anxiety with mechanisms that are historically bound up with it, which, by this very fact, serve merely to augment that anxiety and constantly threaten to arouse it once more. In contrast with the history of the normal individual, the pathological history is marked by this circular monotony.

The psychology of evolution, which describes symptoms as archaic behavior, must be complemented therefore by a psychology of genesis that describes, in a given history, the present meaning of these regressions. A style of psychological coherence must be found that authorizes the understanding of morbid phenomena without taking as its referential model stages described in the manner of biological phases. The nexus of psychological significations must be found on the basis of which, historically, the morbid behavior is ordered.

Now, this point toward which the significations converge is, as we have seen, anxiety. The patient's psychological history is constituted as a set of significative acts that erect defense mechanisms against the ambivalence of affective contradictions. But, in psychological history, the status of anxiety is an ambiguous one: it is anxiety that is to be found beneath the web of all the pathological episodes of a given subject; these episodes are constantly haunted by anxiety; but it is because anxiety was already there that these episodes followed one another, like so many attempts to escape from it; if it accompanied them, it is because it preceded them. Why, in a given situation, does one individual encounter a surmountable conflict and another a contradiction within which he is enclosed in a pathological way? Why is the same Oedipal ambiguity overcome by one individual while, in another, it sets off a long sequence of pathological mechanisms? This is a form of necessity that individual history reveals as a problem but is unable to justify. For a contradiction to be experienced in the anxious mode of ambivalence, for a subject in a conflictual situation to be enclosed in the circularity of pathological defense mechanisms, the anxiety must already be present, having already transformed the ambiguity of a situation into the ambivalence of reactions. If anxiety fills an individual's history, it is because it is its principle and foundation; it defines, from the outset, a certain style of experience that marks the traumas, the psychological mechanisms, that it triggers off, the forms of repetition that it affects in the course of pathological episodes: it is a sort of a priori of existence.

The analysis of evolution situated the illness as a potentiality; the individual history makes it possible to envisage it as a fact of psychological development. But it must now be understood in its existential necessity.

NOTES

1. In "An Autobiographical Study," *The Standard Edition of the Complete Psychological Works of Sigmund Freud,* vol. XX, Freud cites the influence of Darwin on the early orientation of his thought.

2. *Standard Edition,* vol. XVI, pp. 248 ff.

3. *Les origines du caractère chez l'enfant,* p. 217.

4. "Analysis of a Phobia in a Five-Year-Old Boy," *Standard Edition,* vol. X.

5. Anna Freud, *The Ego and the Mechanisms of Defence* (1942), p. 47.

6. *Introductory Lectures on Psycho-Analysis, Standard Edition,* vol. XVI.

7. "The Case of Schreber," *Standard Edition,* vol. XII.

8. Anna Freud, *The Psychoanalytical Treatment of Children* (London, 1946).

9. *Introductory Lectures on Psycho-Analysis, Standard Edition,* vol. XVI, pp. 264 ff.

10. It is this contradictory unity of behavior and affective life that, since Bleuler, has been known as "ambivalence."

4

Mental Illness and Existence

Analysis of the mechanisms of mental illness leaves behind it a reality that supersedes those mechanisms and that constitutes them in their pathological nature; however far that analysis is taken, it invites us to see in anxiety the ultimate morbid element, the heart, as it were, of the illness. But in order to understand anxiety, a new style of analysis is required: a form of experience that goes beyond its own manifestations, anxiety can never be reduced by an analysis of the naturalist type; it is anchored to the heart of individual history, which gives it, beneath all its variations, a single signification; nor can it be exhausted by an analysis of a historical type; but the history and nature of man can be understood only in reference to it.

We must now place ourselves at the center of this experience; it is only by understanding it from the inside that we will be able to set up within the morbid world the natural structures constituted by evolution and the individual mechanisms crystallized by psychological history. A method that owes nothing to the discursive analyses, the mechanistic causality, of the *Naturwissenschaften;* a method that must never turn into biographical history, with its description of successive links and its serial determinism. A method that must, on the contrary, grasp sets of elements as totalities whose elements cannot be dissociated, however dispersed in the history they may be. It is no longer enough to say that the child's fear is the cause of the adolescent's phobias; we must rediscover beneath that original fear and beneath its morbid symptoms the same style of anxiety that gives them their significative unity. Discursive logic is out of place here: it becomes tangled in the threads of delusion and exhausted in an attempt to follow the reasonings of the paranoiac. Intuition goes further and more quickly when it succeeds in restoring the fundamental experience that dominates all pathological processes (in the case of paranoia, for example, the radical alteration of the living relationship with others). At the same time as it reveals in a single gaze essential totalities, intuition reduces, to the point of extinguishing it, the distance that constitutes all objective knowledge: the naturalist analysis envisages the patient with the distance of a natural object; historical reflection preserves him in that alterity that makes possible explanation, but rarely understanding. Intuition, leaping into the interior of morbid consciousness, tries to see the pathological world with the eyes of the patient himself: the truth it seeks is of the order not of objectivity, but of intersubjectivity.

Insofar as comprehension means at once to gather together, to grasp immediately, and to penetrate, this new reflection on mental illness is above all "comprehension" (understanding). It is this method that phenomenological psychology has practiced.

But is it possible to understand everything? Is not the essence of mental illness, as opposed to normal behavior, precisely that it can be explained but that it resists all understanding? Is not jealousy normal when we understand even its most exaggerated forms, and is it not morbid when "we simply can't understand" even its most elementary reactions? It was Jaspers who showed that understanding may be extended beyond the frontiers of the normal and that intersubjective understanding may reach the pathological world in its essence.[1]

There are, no doubt, morbid forms that are still and will remain opaque to phenomenological understanding. There are the direct derivatives of the processes whose very movement is unknown to normal consciousness, like the irruptions in the consciousness of images caused by intoxication, or like those "psychic meteors" that can be explained only by a break in the tempo of the consciousness, by what Jaspers calls a "psychic ataxia"; there are also those impressions that seem to have been borrowed from a sense-material totally alien to our sphere: the feeling of an influence penetrating right into our thinking, an impression of being traversed by fields of forces that are at once material and mysteriously invisible, an experience of an aberrant transformation of the body.

But this side of those distant limits of understanding from which there opens up the, for us, alien, dead world of the insane, the morbid world remains penetrable. It is a question of restoring, through this understanding, both the experience that the patient has of his illness (the way in which he experiences himself as a sick or abnormal individual) and the morbid world on which this consciousness of illness opens, the world at which this consciousness is directed and which it constitutes. The understanding of the sick consciousness and the reconstitution of its pathological world, these are the two tasks of a phenomenology of mental illness.

The consciousness that the patient has of his illness is, strictly speaking, original. Nothing could be more false than the myth of madness as an illness that is unaware of itself as such; the distance between the consciousness of the doctor and the consciousness of the patient is not commensurate with that between the knowledge and ignorance of the illness. The doctor is not on the side of health, possessing all the knowledge about the illness; and the patient is not on the side of the illness, ignorant of everything about it, including its very existence. The patient recognizes his anomaly and it gives him, at least, the sense of an irreducible difference separating him from the world and the consciousness of others. But, however lucid the patient may be, he does not view his illness in the same way the doctor does: he never adopts that speculative distance that would enable him to grasp the illness as an objective process unfolding within him, without his participation; his consciousness of the illness arises from within the illness; it is anchored in it, and at the moment the consciousness perceives the illness, it expresses it. The way in which a subject accepts or rejects his illness, the way in which he interprets it and gives signification to its most absurd forms, constitutes one of the essential dimensions of the illness. It is neither an unconscious collapse within the morbid process nor a lucid, disengaged, objective awareness of this process, but an allusive recognition, the diffuse perception of a morbid setting against the background of which the pathological themes stand out—it is the variations of this mode of ambiguous consciousness that phenomenological reflection must analyze.[2]

1. Illness may be perceived with an objectivity that places the ill consciousness at a maximum distance. In his effort to arrest it and to avoid recognizing himself in it, the patient sees it as an accidental, organic process. The patient maintains his illness at the limits of his body: omitting or denying any alteration in psychological experience, he gives importance to, and in the end, perceives and thematizes, only the organic contents of his experience. Far from hiding his illness, he displays it, but only in its physiological forms; and, in the objectivity that the patient confers on his symptoms, the doctor is right to see the manifestation of subjective disorders. It is this preeminence of the organic processes in the field of the patient's consciousness and in the way in which he apprehends his illness that constitutes the range of hysterical signs (psychogenic paralyses or anesthesias), psychosomatic symptoms, or the hypochondriac worries so often encountered in psychasthenia or certain forms of schizophrenia. As well as being elements of the illness, these organic or pseudo-organic forms are, for the subject, modes of apprehending his illness.

2. In most obsessional disorders, in many cases of paranoia, and in certain schizophrenias, the patient recognizes that the morbid process is at one with his personality. But in a paradoxical way: he rediscovers in his history, in his conflicts with those around him, in the contradictions of his present situation, the premises of his illness; he describes its genesis; but, at the same time, he sees in the beginning of his illness the explosion of a new existence that profoundly alters the meaning of his life, thus becoming a threat to that life. One has only to think of those jealous individuals who justify their mistrust, their interpretations, their delusional systematizations, by a meticulous genesis of their suspicions that seems to dilute their symptoms throughout their existence; but they recognize that, since this or that adventure or this or that emotional upheaval, their whole lives have become transformed, poisoned, unbearable. They see in their morbid jealousy the deepest truth, the most radical misfortune of their existence. They normalize it by referring it to the whole of their previous life, but they detach themselves from it by isolating it as a sudden upheaval. They see their illness as a destiny; it completes their life only by breaking it.

3. This paradoxical unity cannot always be maintained: in such cases, the morbid elements detach themselves from their normal context and, closing upon themselves, constitute an autonomous world—a world that, for the patient, has many of the signs of objectivity: it is promoted and haunted by external forces that, by their very mystery, escape all investigation; its existence is beyond doubt, but it resists all approaches. The hallucinations that fill it give it the perceptible richness of the real; the delusion that unites its elements lends it a quasi-rational coherence. But awareness of the illness is not lost in this quasi objectivity; it remains present, at least in a marginal way: this world of hallucinatory elements and crystallized delusions merely juxtaposes itself with the real world. The patient never confuses his doctor's voice with the hallucinatory voice of his persecutors, even when his doctor is for him no more than a persecutor. The most consistent delusion appears to

the patient just as real as reality itself; and in this interplay of two realities, in this theatrical ambiguity, awareness of the illness reveals itself as awareness of another reality.

The patient is quite willing to recognize this opposition to the real, or rather the irreducible juxtaposition of these two real worlds: a patient suffering from hallucinations asks his interlocutor whether he too hears the voices that pursue him; the patient demands that the doctor accept the evidence of his senses; but if one denies the existence or professes total ignorance of the supposed facts, the patient finds little difficulty in adjusting to this divergence of view and declares that, in that case, he is alone in hearing them. For him, this singularity of experience does not invalidate the certainty that accompanies it; but he recognizes, in accepting it, in affirming it even, the strange, painfully singular character of his universe; by accepting two worlds, by adapting himself to both, he manifests in the background of his behavior a specific awareness of his illness.

4. Lastly, in the ultimate forms of schizophrenia and in the states of dementia, the patient is engulfed in the world of his illness. Yet he grasps the world that he has left as a distant, veiled reality. In this twilight landscape, in which the most real experiences—events, heard words, the people around one—assume a phantomatic appearance, it would seem that the patient still retains an oceanic feeling of his illness. He is submerged in the morbid world and aware of the fact; and, as far as one can guess from the accounts of cured patients, the impression remains ever present to the subject's consciousness that reality can be grasped only in a travestied, caricatured, and metamorphosed, in the strict sense of the term, dream mode. Mme. Séchehaye, who treated and cured a young schizophrenic, collected the impressions experienced by her patient in the course of her pathological episode:

> It was as if my perception of the world made me feel in a more acute form the strangeness of things. In the silence and immensity, each object was cut off by a knife, detached in the void, in limitless space,

separated from other objects. By the very fact of being alone, without any link with the environment, it began to exist. . . . I felt as if I had been thrown out of the world, outside life, as if I were a spectator of some endless, chaotic film in which I couldn't take part.

And a little later she adds: "People appeared to me as in a dream; I could no longer make out their individual characters."[3] The patient's consciousness is then simply an immense moral suffering, confronting a world recognized as such by implicit reference to a reality that has become inaccessible.

Whatever form it takes, and whatever degrees of obnubilation it involves, mental illness always implies a consciousness of illness; the morbid world is never an absolute in which all reference to the normal is suppressed; on the contrary, the sick consciousness is always deployed with, for itself, a double reference, either to the normal and the pathological, or to the familiar and the strange, or to the particular and the universal, or to waking and dream consciousness.

But this sick consciousness cannot be reduced to the consciousness it has of its illness; it is also directed at a pathological world whose structures we must now study, thus complementing the noetic analysis by the noematic analysis.

1. Eugène Minkowski studied disturbances in the temporal forms of the morbid world. In particular, he analyzed a case of paranoid delusion in which the patient felt threatened by catastrophes that no precautions could obviate: at every moment the imminence was renewed, and the fact that the apprehended misfortune never took place could not prove that it would not take place in the next few moments. The catastrophe with which he felt threatened was being crushed to death by all the waste material, dead matter, and garbage in the world. It is easy enough to see a significant relation between this content of delusion and the anxious theme of imminent catastrophe: being haunted by "remains"

expresses, for the subject, an inability to conceive how a thing might disappear, how what is no more cannot but still remain. The accumulation of the past can no longer, for him, be liquidated; and, correlatively, past and present cannot anticipate the future; no acquired security can serve as a guarantee against the threats that it contains; in the future everything is absurdly possible. Thus, in their insane intertwining, these two themes reveal a major disturbance in temporality; time no longer projects itself or flows; the past piles up; and the future, which opens up, can contain as promise only the crushing of the present by the ever increasing weight of the past.

Thus each disorder involves a specific alteration in experienced time.[4] For example, Binswanger, in his *Ideenflucht,* defined the temporal disturbance of mania: time is rendered instantaneous by fragmentation; and, lacking any opening on to the past and future, it spins round upon its axis, proceeding either by leaps or by repetitions. It is against such a background of disturbed temporality that the "flight of ideas," with its characteristic alteration of thematic repetitions of leaping, illogical associations, must be understood. The schizophrenic's time is also subject to interruption, but this occurs through the imminence of the Sudden and the Terrifying, which the patient can escape only through the myth of an empty eternity; the schizophrenic's temporality is thus divided between the fragmented time of anxiety and the formless, contentless eternity of delusion.[5]

2. Space, as a structure of the experienced world, lends itself to the same kind of analysis.

Sometimes distances disappear, as in the case of those delusional subjects who recognize here people they know to be somewhere else, or those subjects suffering from hallucinations who hear their voices, not in the objective space in which sound sources are situated, but in a mythical space, in a sort of quasi space in which the axes of reference are fluid and mobile: they hear next to them, around them, within them, the voices of persecutors, which, at the same time, they situate beyond the walls, beyond the city, beyond all frontiers. The transparent space in which each object has its geographical place and in which perspectives are articulated one upon another is replaced by an opaque space in which objects are mingled together, move forward and away in an immediate mobility, are displaced without movement, and finally fuse in a perspectiveless horizon. As Minkowski says, "clear space" blurs into "obscure space," the space of fear and night; or rather they come together in the morbid world instead of being separated, as in the normal world.[6]

In other cases, space becomes insular and rigid. Objects lose the index of insertion that also marks the possibility of using them; they are offered in a singular plenitude that detaches them from their context, and they are affirmed in their isolation, without any real or potential link with other objects; instrumental relations have disappeared. Roland Kuhn has studied from this angle the delusions of "limits" in certain schizophrenics: the importance given to limits, to frontiers, to walls, to anything that encloses and protects, is a function of the absence of internal unity in the arrangement of things; it is to the extent that things do not "hold" together that they must be protected from the outside and maintained in a unity that is not natural to them. Objects have lost their cohesion and space has lost its coherence, as in the case of the patient who spent his whole time drawing the plan of a fantastic city whose endless fortifications protected only a group of insignificant buildings. The meaning of "utensility" has disappeared from space; for the patient, the world of *Zuhandenen,* to use Heidegger's term, is merely a world of *Vorhandenen.*

3. It is not only the spatiotemporal world, the *Umwelt,* that, in its existential structures, is disturbed by the illness, but also the *Mitwelt,* the social and cultural world. For the patient, others cease to be partners in a dialogue or task; they present themselves to him against the background of social implications, they lose their reality as *socii* and become, in this depopulated world, Strangers. It is to this radical alteration that the frequent syndrome of "symbolic derealization of others" refers—or the feeling of strangeness

when confronted by others' language, systems of expression, bodies; this difficulty in attaining any certainty about others' existence; the heaviness and distance of an inhuman universe in which things freeze when expressed, in which significations have the massive indifference of things, and in which symbols assume the gravity of enigmas: this is the rigid world of the psychasthenic and of most schizophrenics. Mme. Séchehaye's patient described one of her first feelings of unreality thus:

> I found myself in the principal's office; the room suddenly became huge, as if lit up by a terrible light. . . . The pupils and teachers looked like marionettes, moving about aimlessly, with no sense of direction. . . . I listened to the conversations around me, but couldn't catch the words. People's voices seemed metallic, lacking in tone and warmth. From time to time, a single word would stand out from the rest. It would repeat itself in my brain, as if cut off with a knife, absurd.

The child was afraid, the teacher spoke to her, reassuringly:

> She smiled at me kindly. . . . But instead of reassuring me, her smile merely increased my anxiety and confusion; for I became aware of her white, regular teeth. Her teeth gleamed in the bright light and, though I never forgot that they were the teacher's teeth, they soon occupied my whole vision, as if the entire room were nothing but teeth under that pitiless light.[7]

At the other pole of pathology, there is the infinitely fluid world of hallucinatory delusion: a constantly recommenced tumult of pseudorecognitions, in which each other individual is not simply another, but the major Other, constantly re-encountered, constantly pursued and found again; a single presence with the thousand faces of the abhorred man who betrays and kills, of the devouring woman who weaves the great spell of death. Each face, whether strange or familiar, is merely a mask, each statement, whether clear or obscure, conceals only one meaning: the mask of the persecutor and the meaning of persecution.

The masks of psychasthenia, the masks of hallucinatory delusion: it is in the monotony of the first that the variety of human

faces begins to be lost; it is beneath the innumerable profiles of
the second that the delusional experience of the hallucinated subject, single, stable, and burdened with a pitiless meaning, is
rediscovered.

4. Lastly, mental illness may reach man in the individual
sphere in which the experience of his own body takes place. The
body then ceases to be the center of reference around which the
ways of the world open up their possibilities. At the same time, the
presence of the body on the horizon of consciousness alters.
Sometimes it thickens to the point of assuming the heaviness and
immobility of a thing; it veers into an objectivity in which the
consciousness can no longer recognize its *own* body; the subject
experiences himself only as a corpse or as an inert machine, all of
whose impulses emanate from a mysterious exteriority. One of
Eugène Minkowski's patients declared:

> Every other day my body is as hard as wood. Today my body is as thick
> as this wall; all yesterday my body felt as if it were black water, as
> black as this chimney. . . . Everything inside me is black, a sort of
> dirty, frothy black. . . . My teeth are as thick as the side of a drawer.
> . . . My body feels as thick, sticky, and slippery as this parquet floor.[8]

Sometimes, too, the full consciousness of the body, with its
spatiality and the density in which the proprioceptive experiences
are inserted, so declines that it is no more than a consciousness of
an incorporeal life and a delusional belief in an immortal existence; the world of one's own body, the *Eigenwelt,* seems to be
voided of content, and this life, which is simply a consciousness of
immortality, is exhausted in a slow death, which it prepares by the
refusal of all food, all bodily care, and all material concerns.
Binswanger found this disturbance of the *Eigenwelt* in one of his
patients, Ellen West, combined with the loosening of all forms of
insertion in the world. She no longer recognized this mode of
existence, which, within the world, is oriented and moves according to the potential paths traced in space; she no longer knew that
she "had her feet on the ground"; she was caught between the

wish to fly, to float in an etheral jubilation, and the fear of being trapped in a muddy earth that oppressed and paralyzed her. Between joyously instantaneous mobility and the anxiety that engulfed her, the solid, firm space of bodily movement had disappeared; the world had become "silent, icy, dead"; the patient dreamed of her body in terms of a thin, ethereal fluidity that her insubstantiality freed of all materiality. It was this that provided the background of the psychosis and of the symptoms (fear of getting fat, anorexia, affective indifference) that led her over a morbid period of thirteen years to suicide.[9]

One might be tempted to reduce these analyses to historical analyses and to wonder whether what we call the patient's world is not merely an arbitrary section of his history or, at least, the final state in which his development culminates. In fact, although Rudolf, one of Roland Kuhn's patients, remained for many hours beside his mother's corpse while he was still only a small child and was ignorant of the meaning of death, this was not the cause of his illness. Those long contacts with a corpse could have the same meaning as a later necrophilia, and finally an attempted murder, only insofar as a world had been constituted in which death, the corpse, the stiff, cold body, the glassy stare, had acquired a status and a meaning: this world of death and night had first to acquire a privileged place in relation to the world of day and life, and it was necessary that the passage from one to the other, which had previously aroused so much wonder and anxiety in him, should fascinate him so much that he wished to force it, through contact with corpses and through the murder of a woman.[10] The morbid world is not explained by historical causality (I am referring, of course, to psychological history), but historical causality is possible only because this world exists: it is this world that forges the link between cause and effect, the anterior and the ulterior.

But we must examine this notion of "morbid world" and what distinguishes it from the world constituted by the normal man.

Phenomenological analysis no doubt rejects an a priori distinction between normal and pathological: "The validity of phenomenological descriptions is not limited by a judgment on the normal and abnormal."[11] But the morbid manifests itself in the course of investigation as the fundamental characteristic of this world. It is, in effect, a world whose imaginary, not to say oneiric, forms, whose opacity to all the perspectives of intersubjectivity, denounces as a "private world," as an ἴδιον κόσμον; and on the subject of madness Binswanger recalls the words of Heraclitus on sleep: "Those who are awake have a single, common world [ἕνα καὶ κοινὸν κόσμον]; he who sleeps turns toward his own world [εἰς ἴδιον ἀποστρεφε σθαὶ]."[12] But this morbid existence is also marked by a very particular style of abandoning the world: by losing the significations of the world, by losing its fundamental temporality, the subject alienates that existence in the world in which his freedom bursts forth; being unable to possess its meaning, he abandons himself to events; in this fragmented, futureless time, in that incoherent space, one sees the mark of a distintegration that abandons the subject to the world as to an external fate. The pathological process is, as Binswanger says, a *Verweltlichung*. The nucleus of the illness is to be found in this contradictory unity of a private world and an abandonment to the inauthenticity of the world. Or, to use another vocabulary, the illness is both a retreat into the worst of subjectivities and a fall into the worst of objectivities.

But here we may have touched on one of the paradoxes of mental illness that demand new forms of analysis: if this subjectivity of the insane is both a call to and an abandonment of the world, is it not of the world itself that we should ask the secret of its enigmatic status? Is there not in mental illness a whole nucleus of significations that belongs to the domain in which it appeared—and, to begin with, the simple fact that it is in that domain that it is circumscribed *as* an illness?

NOTES

1. K. Jaspers, *General Psychopathology.*
2. It is from this point of view that Wyrsch studied schizophrenia (*Die Person des Schizophrenen*).
3. Séchehaye, *Journal d'une schizophrène*, pp. 50, 56. [*Autobiography of a Schizophrenic Girl*, tr. Grace Rubin-Rabson (New York, 1951). My translation.]
4. Minkowski, *Le temps vécu.*
5. Binswanger, "Der Fall Jurg Zund," *Schweizer Archiv f. Neur. u. Psych.*, 1946.
6. Minkowski, *Le temps vécu.*
7. *Journal d'une schizophrène*, pp. 6-7.
8. In Ajuriaguerra and Hecaen, *Les hallucinations corporelles.*
9. Binswanger, "Der Fall Ellen West," *Schweizer Archiv f. Neur. u. Psych.*, 1943. ["The Case of Ellen West," in *Existence*, ed. Rollo May, Ernest Angel, and Henri F. Ellenberger (New York, 1958).]
10. R. Kuhn, "Mordversuch eines depressiven Fetichisten," *Monatschrift für Psychiatrie*, 1948.
11. *Ibid.*
12. Binswanger, "Traum and Existenz," *Neue Schweizer Runschau*, 1930. ["Dream and Existence," in *Being-in-the-World: Selected Papers of Ludwig Binswanger*, tr. Jacob Needleman (New York, 1963).]

PART II

Madness and Culture

Introduction

The preceding analyses have fixed the coordinates by which psychologies can situate the pathological fact. But although they showed the forms of appearance of the illness, they have been unable to show its conditions of appearance. It would be a mistake to believe that organic evolution, psychological history, or the situation of man in the world may reveal these conditions. It is in these conditions, no doubt, that the illness manifests itself, that its modalities, its forms of expression, its style, are revealed. But the roots of the pathological deviation, as such, are to be found elsewhere.

Using his own vocabulary, Boutroux said that even the most general psychological laws are relative to a "phase of mankind." For a long time now, one fact has become the commonplace of sociology and mental pathology: mental illness has its reality and its value qua illness only within a culture that recognizes it as such. Janet's patient who had visions and who presented stigmata would, in another country, have been a visionary mystic and a worker of miracles. The obsessional who moves in the contagious world of sympathies seems, in his propitiatory gestures, to revive the practices of the primitive magician: the rituals by which he circumvents the object of his obsession assume, for us, a morbid meaning in that belief in taboo with whose equivocal power the

primitive wishes, normally, to be reconciled and of whose danger-
ously favorable complicity he wishes to be assured.
Yet this relativity of the morbid fact is not immediately apparent. Durkheim thought he could account for it by means of a
conception that was both evolutionist and statistical: those
phenomena were regarded as pathological that, by departing from
the average, mark the superseded stages of an earlier evolution or
foreshadow the future stages of a development that has scarcely
begun. "If we agree to call the average type the schematic being
that would be constituted by bringing together in a single whole, in
a sort of abstract universality, the most frequent characteristics of
the species . . . , it might be said that any departure from this
standard of health is a morbid phenomenon"; and he complements
this statistical point of view by adding: "A social fact can be said
to be normal for a given society only in relation to a given stage in
its development" (*Règles de la méthode sociologique*). Despite
very different anthropological implications, the conception of
certain American psychologists is not far removed from Durkheim's point of view. According to Ruth Benedict, each culture
chooses certain of the possibilities that form the anthropological
constellation of man:[1] a particular culture, that of the Kwakiutl, for
example, takes as its theme the exaltation of the individual, while
that of the Zuni radically excludes it; aggression is a privileged
form of behavior in Dobu but repressed among the Pueblos. Each
culture is seen as producing an image of mental illness whose lines
are drawn by the whole set of anthropological possibilities that it
ignores or represses. In his study of the Crow Indians, Lowie cites
the example of one such Indian who possessed an exceptional
knowledge of the cultural forms of his tribe but who was incapable
of confronting physical danger; and in that form of culture that
offers a possibility of expression and attributes value only to
aggressive forms of behavior, his intellectual virtues led him to be
regarded as irresponsible, incompetent, and in the last resort, ill.
"Just as those whose natural reflexes are closest to the behavior
which characterizes their society are favored," says Benedict,

"those whose natural reflexes fall within an arc of behavior which does not exist in their civilization find themselves disoriented." Durkheim's conception and that of the American psychologists' have this in common, that illness is examined from both a negative and a possible point of view. It is negative, since illness is defined in relation to an average, a norm, a "pattern," and since the whole essence of the pathological resides within this departure: illness, it seems, is marginal by nature and relative to a culture only insofar as it is a form of behavior that is not integrated by that culture. It is possible, since the content of mental illness is defined by the possibilities, not in themselves morbid, that are manifested in that culture: for Durkheim, it is the statistical possibility of a departure from the average; for Benedict, it is the anthropological possibility of the human essence; in both analyses, mental illness takes its place among the possibilities that serve as a margin to the cultural reality of a social group.

This, no doubt, is to ignore the positive, real elements in mental illness as it is presented in a society. There are, in effect, illnesses that are recognized as such and that have, within a group, a status and a function; the pathological, then, is no longer simply a deviancy in relation to the cultural type; it is one of the elements and one of the manifestations of this type. Let us leave to one side the celebrated case of the Berdaches, among the Dakota Indians of North America; these homosexuals have a religious status as priests and magicians and an economic role as craftsmen and cultivators bound up with their particular sexual behavior. But there is no indication that their group regards them in any clear way as ill. On the contrary, this consciousness is linked with specific social institutions. This, according to Callaway, is how one becomes a shaman among the Zulus: at first, he who is becoming a shaman

> is sturdy in appearance, but in time he becomes more and more delicate. . . ; he is always complaining of being in pain. . . . He dreams of all kinds of things and his body is muddy. . . . He has convulsions, which cease for a time when water is sprinkled over him.

As soon as he is not shown respect, he bursts into tears and cries noisily. A man who is about to become a wizard is a great cause of trouble.

It would be wrong to say, therefore, that the characteristic forms of behavior of the shaman are possibilities recognized and validated among the Zulus but regarded, on the contrary, as hypochondria or hysteria by Europeans. Not only is the awareness of mental illness not exclusive, here, of the social role, but it even demands the role. Illness, recognized as such, is given a status by the group that denounces it. Other examples could be found in the role played, not so long ago in our societies, by the village idiot and by epileptics.

If Durkheim and the American psychologists have made deviancy and departure the very nature of mental illness, it is no doubt because of a cultural illusion common to both of them: our society does not wish to recognize itself in the ill individual whom it rejects or locks up; as it diagnoses the illness, it excludes the patient. The analyses of our psychologists and sociologists, which turn the patient into a deviant and which seek the origin of the morbid in the abnormal, are, therefore, above all a projection of cultural themes. In fact, a society expresses itself positively in the mental illnesses manifested by its members; and this is so whatever status it gives to these morbid forms: whether it places them at the center of its religious life, as is often the case among primitive peoples; or whether it seeks to expatriate them by placing them outside social life, as does our own culture.

Two questions arise therefore: How did our culture come to give mental illness the meaning of deviancy and to the patient a status that excludes him? And how, despite that fact, does our society express itself in those morbid forms in which it refuses to recognize itself?

NOTE

1. Ruth Benedict, *Patterns of Culture*.

5

The Historical Constitution
of Mental Illness

It was at a relatively recent date that the West accorded madness
the status of mental illness.

It has been said, only too often, that, until the advent of a
positivist medicine, the madman was regarded as someone "possessed." And all histories of psychiatry up to the present day have
set out to show that the madman of the Middle Ages and the
Renaissance was simply an unrecognized mentally ill patient,
trapped within a tight network of religious and magical significations. According to this view, it was only with the arrival of the
calm, objective, scientific gaze of modern medicine that what had
previously been regarded as supernatural perversion was seen as a
deterioration of nature. Such an interpretation is based on a factual
error—that madmen were regarded as possessed; on an inaccurate
prejudice—that people defined as possessed were mentally ill; and
on an error of reasoning—that if the possessed were truly mad, it
followed that madmen were really treated as men possessed. In
fact, the complex problem of possession does not belong directly
to the history of madness, but to the history of religious ideas.
During two periods prior to the nineteenth century, medicine
intervened in the problem of possession. During the first, stretch-

ing from J. Weyer to Duncan (from 1560 to 1640), parliaments, governments, and even the Catholic hierarchy made use of the medical profession in their campaigns against certain monastic orders that were continuing the practices of the Inquisition; doctors were then given the task of showing that all diabolical pacts and rites could be explained in terms of the powers of a disturbed imagination. During the second period, from about 1680 to 1740, the profession was called in by the entire Catholic Church and the government against the explosion of Protestant and Jansenist mysticism unleashed by the persecutions at the end of the reign of Louis XIV; doctors were then called upon by the ecclesiastical authorities to show that all phenomena of ecstasy, inspiration, prophesying, and possession by the Holy Spirit were due (in the case of heretics, of course) simply to the violent movements of the humors or of spirits. The annexation of all these religious or parareligious phenomena by medicine is merely an incidental episode, therefore, in relation to the great work that has defined mental illness; and, above all, it is not the product of an effort essential to the development of medicine; it is religious experience itself that, in order to make up its own mind, appealed, and in a secondary way, to medical confirmation and criticism. It belonged to the destiny of this history that such a criticism should, after the event, be applied by medicine to all religious phenomena and rebound, at the expense of the Catholic Church, which had actually solicited it, against the Christian experience as a whole, and thus show at the same time, and in a paradoxical way, that religion belongs to the fantastic powers of neurosis and that those whom religion had condemned were victims of both their religion and their neurosis. But this rebounding dates only from the nineteenth century, that is, from a period when the definition of mental illness in a positivistic style had already become accepted.

In fact, before the nineteenth century, the experience of madness in the Western world was very polymorphic; and its confiscation in our own period in the concept of "illness" must not deceive us as to its original exuberance. Ever since Greek medicine, part of the domain of madness had no doubt already been concerned with the notions of pathology and with the practices that they involved. In the West, there had always been medical treatment of madness and most of the medieval hospitals had, like the Hôtel-Dieu in Paris, beds reserved for the mad (often in the form of enclosed beds, great cagelike affairs to hold the violent). But these amounted to no more than a small sector, limited to those forms of madness that were regarded as curable ("frenzies," violent episodes, or attacks of "melancholy"). Madness was wide in extension, but it had no medical base.

This extension, however, is not dependent on stable criteria; it varies from period to period, at least as far as its visible dimensions go; it may remain implicit, at water level, as it were; or, on the contrary, it may surface, emerge fully, and become integrated without difficulty in the whole cultural landscape. The end of the fifteenth century was certainly one of those periods in which madness became bound up once more with the essential powers of language. The later manifestations of the Gothic Age were dominated, in turn and in a continuous movement, by the fear of death and the fear of madness. The *Danse macabre* depicted in the Cemetery of the Innocents and the *Triumph of Death* celebrated on the walls of the Campo Santo at Pisa are followed by the innumerable dances and Feasts of Fools that Europe was to celebrate so readily throughout the Renaissance. There were the popular rejoicings around the spectacles put on by the "associations of fools," such as the *Blue Ship* in Flanders; there is a whole iconography extending from Bosch's *Ship of Fools* to Breughel and *Margot la Folle;* there are also the learned texts, the works of philosophy or moral criticism, such as Brant's *Stultifera Navis* or Erasmus's *Praise of Folly*. Lastly, there is the whole literature of madness: the mad scenes in the Elizabethan and French preclassical dramas form part of the dramatic architecture, as do the dreams and, a little later, the recognition scenes: they lead the drama from illusion to truth, from the false solution to the true dénouement. They are one of the essential devices of the baroque theater, as of the novels contemporary with it: the great adventures of the tales of chivalry readily become the extravaganzas of minds that are no longer in control of their fantasies. Shakespeare and Cervantes, at the end of the Renaissance, attest to the great prestige of madness, whose future reign had been announced a hundred years earlier by Brant and Hieronymus Bosch.

This is not to say that the Renaissance did not treat the mad. On the contrary, the fifteenth century saw the opening, first in Spain (at Saragossa), then in Italy, of the first great madhouses. There the mad were subjected to a treatment based very largely no doubt on Arabic medicine. But these were exceptional cases. Generally speaking, madness was allowed free reign; it circulated throughout society, it formed part of the background and language of everyday life, it was for everyone an everyday experience that one sought neither to exalt nor to control. In France, in the early seventeenth century, there were famous madmen who were a great source of entertainment for the public, and the cultivated public at that; some of these, like Bluet d'Arbères, wrote books that were published and read as works of madness. Up to about 1650, Western culture was strangely hospitable to these forms of experience.

About the middle of the seventeenth century, a sudden change took place: the world of madness was to become the world of exclusion.

Throughout Europe, great internment houses were created with the intention of receiving not simply the mad, but a whole series of individuals who were highly different from one another, at least according to our criteria of perception—the poor and disabled, the elderly poor, beggars, the work-shy, those with venereal diseases, libertines of all kinds, people whose families or the royal power wished to spare public punishment, spendthrift fathers, defrocked priests; in short, all those who, in relation to the order of reason, morality, and society, showed signs of "derangement." It was in this spirit that the government opened, in Paris, the Hôpital Général, with Bicêtre and La Salpêtrière; some time earlier, St. Vincent de Paul had turned the old lazar house of Saint-Lazare into a prison of this kind, and soon Charenton, originally a hospital, was remodeled on these new institutions. In France, every town of any size was to have its Hôpital Général.

These houses had no medical vocation; one was not admitted in order to receive treatment; one was taken in because one could no longer cope with life or because one was no longer fit to belong to society. The internment to which the madman, together with many others, was subjected in the classical period concerns not the relations between madness and illness, but the relations between society and itself, between society and what it recognized and did not recognize in the behavior of individuals. Internment was no doubt a form of public assistance; the numerous foundations from which it benefited are proof of this. But it was a system whose ideal was entirely enclosed upon itself: at the Hôpital Général, as in the workhouses in Britain, which were more or less contemporary, forced labor was the rule; a variety of objects were spun, woven, or manufactured that were put on the market cheaply, thus helping the hospital to pay its way. But the compulsion to work also had the role of a sanction, of moral control. In the bourgeois world then being constituted, the major vice, the cardinal sin in that world of trade, had been defined; it was no longer, as in the Middle Ages, pride or greed, but sloth. The common category that grouped together all those interned in these institutions was their inability to participate in the production, circulation, or accumulation of wealth (whether or not through any fault of their own). The exclusion to which they were subjected goes hand in hand with that inability to work, and it indicates the appearance in the modern world of a caesura that had not previously existed. Internment, therefore, was linked, in its origin and in its fundamental meaning, with this restructuring of social space.

This phenomenon was doubly important for the constitution of the contemporary experience of madness. Firstly, because madness, which had for so long been overt and unrestricted, which had

for so long been present on the horizon, disappeared. It entered a
phase of silence from which it was not to emerge for a long time; it
was deprived of its language; and although one continued to speak
of it, it became impossible for it to speak of itself. Impossible at
least until Freud, who was the first to open up once again the
possibility for reason and unreason to communicate in the danger
of a common language, ever ready to break down and disintegrate
into the inaccessible. On the other hand, madness, in internment,
had forged strange new kinships. This space of exclusion, which
had grouped together, with the mad, sufferers from venereal
diseases, libertines, and innumerable major or petty criminals,
brought about a sort of obscure assimilation; and madness forged a
relationship with moral and social guilt that it is still perhaps not
ready to break. We should not be surprised that, since the eighteenth century, a link should have been discovered between madness and all *crimes passionels;* that, since the nineteenth century,
madness should have become the heir of crimes that find in it their
reason for being and their reason for not being crimes; that, in the
twentieth century, madness should have discovered at the center of
itself a primitive nucleus of guilt and aggression. All this is not the
gradual discovery of the true nature of madness, but simply the
sedimentation of what the history of the West has made of it for the
last three hundred years. Madness is much more *historical* than is
usually believed, and much *younger* too.

Internment retained its initial function of silencing madness for
hardly more than a century. From the middle of the eighteenth
century, anxiety once more raised its head. The madman reap-
peared in the most familiar landscapes; he was to be found once
again participating in everyday life. *Le neveu de Rameau* is evidence of this. This was because at this period the world of internment—a world that madness shared with so many offenses and
crimes—began to break up. Political denunciation of arbitrary
confinements, economic criticism of the foundations and the tradi-

tional form of assistance, and popular fear of institutions like
Bicêtre or Saint-Lazare, which came to be regarded as hotbeds of
evil, combined to produce a universal demand for the abolition of
internment. Restored to its former freedom, what was to become
of madness?

The pre-1789 reformers and the Revolution itself wished to
abolish internment as a symbol of ancient oppression and, at the
same time, to restrict hospital assistance as far as possible on the
grounds that it was a sign of the existence of a penurious class.
Attempts were made to define a formula of financial help and
medical care from which the poor would benefit at home, thus
being relieved of their fear of the hospital. But the special factor
involved where the mad are concerned is that they may become
dangerous for their families and for the groups in which they live.
Hence the need to contain them and the penal sanction inflicted on
those who allow "madmen and dangerous animals" to roam
freely.

It was to resolve this problem that, under the Revolution and the
Empire, the old houses of internment were gradually used for the
confinement of the mad, but this time for the *mad alone.* Those
whom the philanthropy of the period had freed were therefore all
the others *except* the mad; the mad came to be the natural
inheritors of internment, the privileged titulars of the old measures
of exclusion.

Internment no doubt took on a new signification at this point: it
assumed a medical character. Pinel in France, Tuke in England,
and Wagnitz and Reil in Germany lent their names to this reform.
And virtually every history of psychiatry or medicine has seen in
these figures the symbols of a double advent: that of a humanism
and that of a science that had at last achieved a positive status.

In fact, things were quite otherwise. Pinel, Tuke, and their
contemporaries and successors did not relax the old practices of
internment; on the contrary, they tightened them around the madmen. The ideal asylum that Tuke created near York was supposed
to reconstruct around the internee a family-like structure in which

he would feel at home; in fact, he was subjected, by that same structure, to uninterrupted social and moral supervision; curing him was to mean reinculcating in him the feelings of dependence, humility, guilt, and gratitude that are the moral backbone of family life. To achieve this end, such means as threats, punishment, deprivation of food, and humiliation were used; in short, whatever might both *infantilize* the madman and *make him feel guilty*. At Bicêtre, Pinel used similar techniques, after having "freed the prisoners" who still remained there in 1793. Certainly, he freed the mentally ill of the material bonds (though not all of them) that physically restricted them. But he reconstituted around them a whole network of moral chains that transformed the asylum into a sort of perpetual court of law: the madman was to be supervised in his every movement, to have all his pretensions shattered, his ravings contradicted, and his mistakes ridiculed; sanctions were immediately applied to any departure from normal behavior. All this took place under the direction of a doctor whose task was not so much that of therapeutic intervention as that of ethical supervision. Within the asylum, he was the agent of moral synthesis.

But there is more to it than this. Despite the very great extent of the internment measures, the classical age allowed the medical treatment of madness to survive and even, to some extent, develop. In the ordinary hospitals, there were special sections for the mad, where they were given treatment; and the medical texts of the seventeenth and eighteenth centuries set out to define, especially with the great multiplication of "vapors" and nervous diseases, the most appropriate techniques for the cure of the mad. These treatments were neither psychological nor physical: they were both at once—the Cartesian distinction between extension and thought had not yet affected the unity of medical practices; the patient was subjected to showers and baths in order to refresh both the spirits and the fibers of his body; he was injected with fresh blood in order to renew a defective circulation; attempts were made to alter the course of his imagination by arousing vivid impressions in him.

However, these techniques, which were justified by the physiology of the period, were taken up by Pinel and his successors in a purely repressive and moral context. The shower was used not to refresh, but to punish; it was applied not when the patient was "overheated," but when he had misbehaved; well into the nineteenth century, Leuret was subjecting his patients to icy showers on the head while, at the same time, conducting a dialogue with them in which he tried to compel them to admit that their beliefs were simply the product of delusion. The eighteenth century had also invented a rotating machine on which the patient was placed so that the free course of his mind, which had become too fixated on some delusional idea, should be set in motion once more and rediscover its natural circuits. The nineteenth century perfected the system by giving it a strictly punitive character: At every delusional manifestation the patient was turned until he fainted, or until he came to his senses. A mobile cage was also developed that turned horizontally on its axis and that moved in accordance with the patient's own degree of agitation. All these medical games are asylum versions of old techniques based on an abandoned physiology. The essential fact is that the asylum founded for internment in Pinel's time represented not the "medicalization" of a social space of exclusion, but the confusion within a single moral regime of techniques of which some were in the nature of a social precaution, while others had the character of a medical strategy.

It was about this time that madness ceased to be regarded as an overall phenomenon affecting, through the imagination and delusion, both body and soul. In the new world of the asylum, in that world of a punishing morality, madness became a fact concerning essentially the human soul, its guilt, and its freedom; it was now inscribed within the dimension of interiority; and by that fact, for the first time in the modern world, madness was to receive psychological status, structure, and signification. But this psychologization was merely the superficial consequence of a more obscure, more deeply embedded operation—an operation by which madness was insered in the system of moral values and repressions. It was enclosed in a punitive system in which the madman, reduced to the status of a minor, was treated in every way as a child, and in which madness was associated with guilt and wrongdoing. It is hardly surprising, then, that an entire psychopathology—beginning with Esquirol, but including our own—should be governed by the three themes that define its problematic: the relations of freedom to the complusions, the phenomena of regression and the infantile structure of behavior, aggression and guilt. What one discovers under the name of the "psychology" of madness is merely the result of the operations by which one has invested it. None of this psychology would exist without the *moralizing sadism* in which nineteenth-century "philanthropy" enclosed it, under the hypocritical appearances of "liberation."

It might be said that all knowledge is linked to the essential forms of cruelty. The knowledge of madness is no exception. Indeed, in the case of madness, this link is no doubt of particular importance. Because it was first of all this link that made possible a psychological analysis of madness; but above all because it was on this link that the possibility of any psychology was secretly based. It must not be forgotten that "objective," or "positive," or "scientific" psychology found its historical origin and its basis in pathological experience. It was an analysis of duplications that made possible a psychology of the personality; an analysis of compulsions and of the unconscious that provided the basis for a psychology of consciousness; an analysis of deficits that led to a psychology of intelligence. In other words, man became a "psychologizable species" only when his relation to madness made a psychology possible, that is to say, when his relation to madness was defined by the external dimension of exclusion and punishment and by the internal dimension of moral assignation and guilt. In situating madness in relation to these two fundamental axes, early - nineteenth - century man made it possible to *grasp* madness and thus to initiate a general psychology.

This experience of Unreason in which, up to the eighteenth century, Western man encountered the night of his truth and its absolute challenge was to become, and still remains for us, the mode of access to the natural truth of man. It is understandable, then, that this mode of access should be so ambiguous and that, at the same time, it invites objective reductions (on the side of *exclusion*) and constantly solicits the recall to self (on the side of *moral assignation*). The whole epistemological structure of contemporary psychology is rooted in this event, which is contemporary with the French Revolution and which concerns man's relation with himself. "Psychology" is merely a thin skin on the surface of the ethical world in which modern man seeks his truth—and loses it. Nietzsche, who has been accused of saying the contrary, saw this very clearly.

As a result, a psychology of madness cannot but be derisory, and yet it touches on the essential. It is derisory because, in wishing to carry out a psychology of madness, one is demanding that psychology should undermine its own conditions, that it should turn back to that which made it possible, and that it should circumvent what is for it, by definition, the unsupersedable. Psychology can never tell the truth about madness because it is madness that holds the truth of psychology. And yet a psychology of madness cannot fail to move toward the essential, since it is obscurely directed toward the point at which its possibilities are created; that is to say, it moves upstream against its own current toward those regions in which man has a relation with himself and inaugurates that form of alienation that turns him into *Homo psychologicus*. If carried back to its roots, the psychology of madness would appear to be not the mastery of mental illness and hence the possibility of its disappearance, but the destruction of psychology itself and the discovery of that essential, nonpsychological because nonmoralizable relation that is the relation between Reason and Unreason.

It is this relation that, despite all the penury of psychology, is present and visible in the works of Hölderlin, Nerval, Roussel, and

Artaud, and that holds out the promise to man that one day, perhaps, he will be able to be free of all psychology and be ready for the great tragic confrontation with madness.

6

Madness: An Overall Structure

What has just been said is not intended as an a priori criticism of any attempt to circumscribe the phenomena of madness or to define a strategy of cure. It was intended simply to show a particular relation between psychology and madness and a disequilibrium so fundamental that they rendered vain any attempt to treat the whole of madness, the essence and nature of madness, in terms of psychology. The very notion of "mental illness" is the expression of an attempt doomed from the outset. What is called "mental illness" is simply *alienated madness,* alienated in the psychology that it has itself made possible.

One day an attempt must be made to study madness as an overall structure—madness freed and disalienated, restored in some sense to its original language.

At first sight, it would no doubt appear that there is no culture that is not aware, in the behavior and language of men, of certain phenomena in regard to which society takes up a particular stance: these men are treated neither entirely as madmen, nor entirely as criminals, nor entirely as witches, nor entirely as ordinary people.

There is something in them that speaks of difference and demands differentiation. Let us avoid saying that it is the first consciousness, obscure and diffuse, of what our scientific spirit recognizes as mental illness; it is simply the void within which the experience of madness resides. But beneath this purely negative form a positive relation is already being forged in which society puts its values at risk. Thus the Renaissance, after the great terror of death, the fear of the apocalypses, and the threats of the other world, experienced a new danger in this world: that of a silent invasion from within, a secret gap in the earth, as it were. This invasion is that of the Insane, which places the Other world on the same level as this one, and on ground level, as it were. As a result, one no longer knows whether it is our world that is duplicated in a fantastic mirage; whether, on the contrary, it is the other world that takes possession of this world; or whether the secret of *our* world was to be already, without our knowing, the *other* world. This uncertain, ambiguous experience that allows strangeness to reside at the very heart of the familiar assumes with Hieronymus Bosch the style of the visible: the world is peopled in all its shells, in each of its herbs, with tiny disturbing, pitiful monsters that are at once truth and lies, illusion and secret, the Same and the Other. *The Garden of Earthly Delights* is not the symbolic, concerted image of madness nor the spontaneous projection of a delusional imagination; it is the perception of a world sufficiently near to, and sufficiently far from, self to be open to the absolute difference of the Insane. Faced with this threat, Renaissance culture put its values to the test and engaged them in combat in a way that was more ironic than tragic. Reason, too, recognized itself as being duplicated and dispossessed of itself: it thought itself wise, and it was mad; it thought it knew, and it knew nothing; it thought itself righteous, and it was insane; knowledge led one to the shades and to the forbidden world, when one thought one was being led by it to eternal light. A whole "play" took shape that dominated the Renaissance: not the skeptical play of a reason that recognizes its

limits, but the more severe, more risky, more seriously ironic play
of a reason that plays its part with the Insane.

Against the background of these very general, primitive experiences, others were taking shape that were already more articulated. These were positive and negative valuations, forms of
acceptance and refusal concerning the experiences we have been
discussing. It is clear that the sixteenth century valued and recognized what the seventeenth century was to misunderstand,
devalue, and reduce to silence. Madness in the widest sense was
situated there: at that level of sedimentation in the phenomena of
culture in which the negative appraisal began of what had been
originally apprehended as the Different, the Insane, Unreason. It is
there that moral significations are engaged and defenses come into
play; barriers are erected and all the rituals of exclusion organized.
These exclusions may vary according to different types of culture:
geographical separation (as in those Indonesian societies in which
the "different" man lives alone, sometimes a few miles away
from the village), material separation (as in our societies, with
their practice of internment), or simply potential separation,
scarcely visible from the outside (as in early-seventeenth-century
Europe).

These tactics of separation serve as a framework for the perception of madness. The recognition that enables one to say, "This
man is mad," is neither a simple nor an immediate act. It is based
in fact on a number of earlier operations and above all on the
dividing up of social space according to the lines of valuation and
exclusion. When the doctor thinks he is diagnosing madness as a
phenomenon of nature, it is the existence of this threshold that
enables him to make such a judgment. Each culture has its own
threshold, which evolves with the configuration of that culture;
since the mid-nineteenth century, the threshold of sensitivity to
madness has considerably lowered in our society; the existence of
psychoanalysis is evidence of this lowering in that it is an effect as
well as a cause of it. It should be noted that this threshold is not

necessarily linked to the acuteness of medical consciousness: the
madman may be perfectly recognized and isolated, yet have no
precise pathological status, as was the case in Europe before the
nineteenth century.

Linked with the level of the threshold but relatively independent
of it, there is the factor of tolerance to the very existence of the
madman. In present-day Japan, the proportion of madmen recognized as such by those around them is practically the same as in the
United States; but, in the West, there is a high level of intolerance,
in that the social group (basically the family) is incapable of
integrating or even of accepting the deviant person; hospitalization
or simply separation from the family is immediately demanded. In
Japan, on the other hand, the environment is much more tolerant
and hospitalization is far from being the rule. One of the many
reasons that lower the number of admissions to European asylums
during wars and serious crises is that the level of the integrative
norms of the environment falls sharply, with the result that the
society becomes much more tolerant than in ordinary times, when
it is more coherent and under less pressure from events.

It is on the basis constituted by these four levels that a medical
consciousness of madness then becomes a recognition of illness.
But there is nothing to compel a diagnosis of "mental" illness.
Neither Arabic, medieval, nor even post-Cartesian medicine
accepted the distinction between illnesses of the body and illnesses
of the mind; each pathological form involved man in his totality.
And the organization of a psychopathology still presupposes a
whole series of operations that, on the one hand, make possible the
division into organic pathology and the knowledge of mental
illnesses, and that, on the other hand, define the laws of a
"metapathology" common to the two domains whose phenomena
it abstractly governs. This theoretical organization of mental illness is bound up with a whole system of practices: the organization
of the medical network, the system of detection and prophylaxis,
the type of assistance, the distribution of treatment, the criteria of

cure, the definition of the patient's civil incapacity and of his penal irresponsibility: in short, a whole set of practices that defines the concrete life of the madman in a given society.

But these practices are merely an indication of all the distances maintained by a society with regard to this major experience of the Insane, which, gradually, through successive divisions, becomes *madness, illness,* and *mental illness.* The contrary movement should also be shown, that is to say, that movement by which a culture comes to express itself, positively, in the phenomena it rejects. Even when silenced and excluded, madness has value as a language, and its contents assume meaning, on the basis of that which denounces and rejects it as madness. Let us take the example of mental illness with all the structures and patterns that our psychology appears to recognize in it.

Mental illness is situated in evolution as a disturbance of the latter's course; through its repressive aspect, it reveals infantile behavior or archaic forms of the personality. But evolutionism is wrong to see in these returns the very essence of the pathological and its real origin. If regression to childhood is manifested in neuroses, it is so merely as an effect. In order for infantile behavior to be a refuge for the patient, for its reappearance to be regarded as an irreducible pathological fact, a society must establish a margin between the individual's present and past that cannot and must not be crossed; a culture must integrate the past only by forcing it to disappear. And this is certainly a feature of our own culture. When, with Rousseau and Pestallozzi, the eighteenth century concerned itself with constituting for the child, with educational rules that followed his development, a world that would be adapted to him, it made it possible to form around children an unreal, abstract, archaic environment that had no relation to the adult world. The whole development of contemporary education, with its irreproachable aim of preserving the child from adult conflicts, accentuates the distance that separates, for a man, his life as a child and his life as an adult. That is to say, by sparing the child conflicts, it exposes him to a major conflict, to the contradiction between his childhood and his real life.[1] If one adds that, in its educational institutions, a culture does not project its reality directly, with all its conflicts and contradictions, but that it reflects it indirectly through the myths that excuse it, justify it, and idealize it in a chimerical coherence; if one adds that in its education a society dreams of its golden age (one has only to remember those of Plato and Rousseau, Durkheim's republican institution, the educational naturalism of the Weimar Republic), one understands that fixations and pathological regressions are possible only in a given culture, that they multiply to the extent that social forms do not permit the assimilation of the past into the present content of experience. Neuroses of regression do not reveal the neurotic nature of childhood, but they denounce the archaizing character of the institutions concerned with childhood. What serves as a background to these pathological forms is the conflict, within a society, between the forms of education of the child, in which the society hides its dreams, and the conditions it creates for adults, in which its real present, with all its miseries, can be read. The same might be said of cultural development: religious delusions, with their system of assertions and the magical horizon that they always imply, are offered as individual regressions in relation to social development. It is not that religion is delusional by nature, nor that the individual, beyond present-day religion, rediscovers his most suspect psychological origins. But religious delusion is a function of the secularization of culture: religion may be the object of delusional belief insofar as the culture of a group no longer permits the assimilation of religious or mystical beliefs in the present content of experience. To this conflict and to the need to overcome it belong the messianic delusions, the hallucinatory experience of apparitions, and the evidences of the thunderous "call" that restore, in the world of madness, the shattered unity experienced in the real world. The historical horizon of psychological regressions is therefore in a conflict of cultural themes, each marked by a chronological index revealing their diverse historical origins. Individual history, with its traumas, its defense mechanisms, and, above all, the anxiety that haunts it, seemed to form another of the psychological dimensions of illness. Psychoanalysis has placed at the origin of these conflicts a "metapsychological" debate, at the frontiers of mythology ("the instincts are our myths," Freud himself said), between the life instinct and the death instinct, between pleasure and repetition, between Eros and Thanatos. But this is to erect into a form of solution what is confronted in the problem. If illness finds a privileged mode of expression in this interweaving of contradictory acts, it is not because the elements of the contradiction are juxtaposed, as segments of conflict, in the human unconscious, but simply because man makes of man a contradictory experience. The social relations that determine a culture, in the form of competition, exploitation, group rivalry, or class struggle, offer man an experience of his human environment that is permanently haunted by contradiction. The system of economic relations attaches him to others, but through negative links of dependence; the laws of coexistence that unite him to his fellow men in a common fate set him in opposition to them in a struggle that, paradoxically, is merely the dialectical form of those laws; the universality of economic and social links enables him to recognize, in the world, a fatherland and to read a common signification in the gaze of every man, but this signification may also be that of hostility, and that fatherland may denounce him as a foreigner. Man has become for man the face of his own truth as well as the possibility of his death. Only in the imaginary can he recognize the fraternal status in which his social relations find their stability and coherence: others always offer themselves in an experience that the dialectic of life and death renders precarious and perilous. The Oedipus complex, the nexus of familial ambivalences, is like the reduced version of this contradiction: the child does not himself bring this love-hate that binds him to his parents; he meets it only in the adult world, specified by the attitude of parents who implicitly discover in their own behavior the old theme that the life of children is the death of parents. Moreover, it is no accident that Freud, reflecting on the neuroses of war, should have discovered, as a counterweight for the life instinct, in which the old European optimism of the eighteenth century was still expressed, a death instinct, which introduced into psychology for the first time the power of the negative. Freud wished to explain war; but it was war that was dreamed in this shift in Freud's thinking. Or, rather, our culture was experiencing at that time, in a way that was clear for itself, its own contradictions: man had to renounce the old dream of solidarity and admit that he could and must experience himself negatively, through hate and aggression. Psychologists have called this experience "ambivalence" and have seen it as a conflict of instincts. A mythology built on so many dead myths.

Lastly, morbid phenomena seemed, in their convergence, to designate a unique structure of the pathological world; and this world seems to offer, on phenomenological examination, the paradox of being, at one and the same time, the inaccessible "private world" to which the patient withdraws in favor of an arbitrary existence of fantasy and delusion, and the world of constraint to which he is doomed through abandonment; this contradictory projection would seem to be one of the essential movements of mental illness. But this pathological form is merely secondary in relation to the real contradiction that causes it. The determinism that sustains it is not the magical causality of a consciousness fascinated by its world, but the effective causality of a world that cannot, of itself, offer a solution to the contradictions that it has given rise to. If the world projected in the fantasy of delusion imprisons the consciousness that projects it, it is not because consciousness itself becomes trapped in it or because consciousness divests itself of its possibilities of being; it is because, in alienating consciousness' freedom, the world cannot acknowledge its madness. In opening itself up to a delusional world, it is not by means of an imaginary constraint that the morbid consciousness is attached; but in submitting to real constraint, it escapes into a morbid world in which it rediscovers, without recognizing it, the same real constraint: for it is not by wishing to escape it that one goes beyond reality. A great deal has been said about contemporary madness and its connection with the world of the machine and the disappearance of direct affective relations between men. This connection is, no doubt, a true one, and it is no accident that today the morbid world takes on the appearance of a world in which mechanistic rationality excludes the continuous spontaneity of the affective life. But it would be absurd to say that the sick man machinizes his world because he projects a schizophrenic world in which he is lost; it is even untrue to say that he is a schizophrenic, because this is the only way open to him of escaping from the constraints of his real world. In fact, when man remains alienated from what takes place in his language, when he cannot recognize any human, living signification in the productions of his activity, when economic and social determinations place constraints upon him and he is unable to feel at home in this world, he lives in a culture that makes a pathological form like schizophrenia possible; a stranger in a real world, he is thrown back upon a "private world" that can no longer be assured of objectivity; subjected, however, to the constraints of this real world, he experiences the world in which he is fleeing as his fate. The contemporary world makes schizophrenia possible, not because its events render it inhuman and abstract, but because our culture reads the world in such a way that man himself cannot recognize himself him in it. Only the real conflict of the conditions of existence may serve as a structural model for the paradoxes of the schizophrenic world.

To sum up, it might be said that the psychological dimensions of mental illness cannot, without recourse to sophistry, be regarded as autonomous. To be sure, mental illness may be situated in relation to human genesis, in relation to individual, psychological history, in relation to the forms of existence. But, if one is to avoid resorting to such mythical explanations as the evolution of psychological structures, the theory of instincts, or an existential anthropology, one must not regard these various aspects of mental illness as ontological forms. In fact, it is only in history that one can discover the sole concrete a priori from which mental illness draws, with the empty opening up of its possibility, its necessary figures.

NOTE

1. It is perhaps in this heterogeneity and in the margin that separates these two forms of life that the root of this phenomenon, which Freud described as the latency period and which he connected with a mythical retreat of the libido, is to be found.

Conclusion

I have purposely not referred to the physiological and anatom-
icopathological problems concerning mental illness or to those
concerning techniques of cure. It is not that psychopathological
analysis is independent, de facto or de jure, of them; recent
discoveries about the physiology of the diencephalic centers and
their regulatory role on the affective life, or the ever increasing
knowledge that we have gained since the early experiences of
Breuer and Freud through the development of psychoanalytic
strategy, would be enough to prove the contrary. But neither
physiology nor therapeutics can become those absolute viewpoints
from which the psychology of mental illness can be resolved or
eliminated. After about one hundred and forty years, ever since
Bayle discovered the specific lesions of general paralysis and
found fairly frequent "delusions of grandeur" in the initial stages
of his symptomatology, we still do not know why it is precisely a
hypomanic exaltation that accompanies such lesions. And
although the success of psychoanalytic intervention is one with the

discovery of the "truth" of the neurosis, it uncovers it only within the new psychological drama in which it is caught up.

The psychological dimensions of madness cannot, therefore, be eliminated on the basis of a principle of explanation or reduction external to them. They must be situated within the general relation that Western man established between himself and himself close on two hundred years ago. Seen from its most acute angle, this relation is the psychology in which he has put a little of his astonishment, much of his pride, and most of his ability to forget; seen from a wider angle, it is the emergence, in the forms of knowledge, of a *Homo psychologicus,* possessor of internal truth, fleshless, ironical, and positive of all self-consciousness and all possible knowledge; lastly, when seen from the widest angle, this relation is that which man has substituted for his relation to truth, by alienating it in the fundamental postulate that he is himself the truth of the truth.

This relation, which is the philosophical foundation of all possible psychology, could be defined only from a particular moment in the history of our civilization: the moment at which the great confrontation between Reason and Unreason ceased to be waged in the dimension of freedom, and in which reason ceased to be for man an ethic and became a nature. Madness then became a nature of nature, that is to say, a process alienating nature, binding it in its determinism; while freedom also became a nature of nature, but in the sense of a secret soul, an inalienable essence of nature. And man, instead of being placed before the great divide of the Insane and in the dimension that it inaugurated, became, at the level of his natural being, *both* madness and freedom, thus acquiring, by virtue of his essence, the right to be both a nature of nature and a truth of truth.

There is a very good reason why psychology can never master madness; it is because psychology became possible in our world only when madness had already been mastered and excluded from the drama. And when, in lightning flashes and cries, it reappears, as in Nerval or Artaud, Nietzsche or Roussel, it is psychology that remains silent, *speechless,* before this language that borrows a meaning of its own from that tragic split, from that freedom, that, for contemporary man, only the existence of "psychologists" allows him to forget.

SOME DATES IN THE HISTORY
OF PSYCHIATRY

1793 PINEL becomes physician-in-chief at the mental institution of Bicêtre.

1822 BAYLE's thesis, *Recherches sur les maladies mentales* (definition of general paralysis).

1838 Law on the insane.

1843 BAILLARGER founds the *Annales médico-psychologiques.*

1884 JACKSON, *Croonian Lectures.*

1889 KRAEPELIN, *Lehrbuch der Psychiatrie.*

1890 MAGNAN, *La folie intermittante.*

1893 BREUER and FREUD, *Studies on Hysteria.*

1894 JANET, *L'automatisme psychologique.*

1909 FREUD, "Analysis of a Phobia in a Five-Year-Old Boy."

1911 FREUD, "Psycho-Analytic Notes on an Autobiographical Account of a Case of Paranoia" ("The Case of Schreber").

1911 BLEULER, *Dementia Praecox, or the Group of Schizophrenias.*

1913 JASPERS, *General Psychopathology.*

1921 FREUD, *Beyond the Pleasure Principle.*

1926 PAVLOV, *Conditioned Reflexes: An Investigation of the Physiological Activity of the Cerebral Cortex.*

1928   MONAKOW and MOURGUE, *Introduction biologique à l'étude de la neurologie et de la psychopathologie.*

1933   L. BINSWANGER, *Über Ideenflucht.*

1936   Egas MONIZ carries out the first lobotomies.

1938   CERLETTI begins the use of electric-shock treatment.